Miss Betsey

Miss Betsey
A Memoir of Marriage

Eugene D. Genovese

Wilmington, Delaware

In Loving Memory of a Great Lady

Elizabeth Ann Fox was born May 28, 1941. Her father insisted on calling her "Betsey," spelled with two e's. She died at age sixty-five on January 2, 2007, as Elizabeth Ann Teresa Fox-Genovese. "Betsey" to the End.

[Betsey] understood and lived the promise of our Lord: "You shall know the truth, and the truth shall set you free." Given the temper and difficulty of our times, she also understood what Flannery O'Connor is said to have added: "You will know the truth, and the truth will make you odd." Betsey was not afraid to face the consequences or responsibilities of the truth.

—Msgr. Richard Lopez,
funeral sermon

Genovese, Eugene D., 1930–

    Miss Betsey : a memoir of marriage / Eugene D. Genovese.—1st ed. —Wilmington, Del. : ISI Books, c2009.

        p. ; cm.
        ISBN: 978-1-935191-01-8
        Includes index.

        1. Fox-Genovese, Elizabeth, 1941–2007. 2. Married people—United States—Biography. 3. Historians—United States—Biography. 4. Feminists—United States—Biography. I. Title.

CT275.F694 G46 2009   2008940175

920/.073—dc22   0904

Published in the United States by:
ISI Books
Intercollegiate Studies Institute
3901 Centerville Road
Wilmington, DE 19807-0431
wwww.isibooks.org

Book design by Beer Editorial and Design
Manufactured in the United States of America

Contents

Apologia

*And I will bring the blind by a way that they knew not; I will lead
them in paths that they have not known: I will make darkness light
before them, and crooked things straight. These things will I do unto
them, and not forsake them.*

—Isaiah 42:16

Montreal, 1967. A vibrant city. Ideal for a twice-divorced man in
his thirties. In 1945, at age fifteen, I left the Catholic Church
for the Communist movement, losing interest in the Command-
ments of a God who—I knew perfectly well—did not exist. Twenty-
two years later, I moved to Montreal as a professor of history at Sir
George Williams University. As I had done during my years in New
York, I worked mostly at home. Hence, I spent a large part of my modest income on comfortable quarters: a three-and a-half room apartment with two bathrooms, a small balcony, and wall space for my
growing library.

In the days before television, radio comics had sport with the
come-on of the era: "Come up and see my etchings." Growing up in a

working-class neighborhood in Brooklyn, I did not have the slightest idea of what etchings were. I did not find out until I attended Brooklyn College in 1948. Not that it mattered. I could not afford etchings anyway, and by the 1950s they no longer qualified as a plausible come-on. I discovered an irresistible alternative in Montreal, which was freezing much of the year. My high-rise had an enclosed rooftop with a large heated swimming pool and sauna. So you cannot fairly rebuke young ladies who succumbed to the lure.

I lived an academic workaholic's dream. At my desk comfortably before seven a.m., I worked until ten p.m. or later and then enjoyed the company of one or another pretty, charming, bright young lady who dropped by for a nightcap. I limited my welcome for each to once a week, which was about the amount of time any of them seemed to need me as a break from more promising adventures. Simply marvelous! Today we would, I suppose, say, "Cool!" I had a "swinging lifestyle"—as the modish call promiscuity and self-indulgence.

The swinging that sounds wildly exciting in the telling proved dreary in the living. Pretending to enjoy every minute of a life that, to be sure, had momentary pleasures, I found it not so much repulsive as bleak. My professional career as a historian was doing well, and the New York literati showered me with plaudits, if only for a few years. Unfortunately, the New York literati had few charms for me and swinging had fewer. I wanted nothing so much as a quiet married home life. My two marital failures beset me with bad memories and revulsion at my bad judgment. I did not deceive myself about my prospects. A two-time loser, I knew that a third marriage would have to be my last—one way or the other.

When I met Betsey in 1968, I was a jaded thirty-eight, she a buoyant twenty-seven despite poor health. By the grace of God I entered into the life I had always hoped to have. My life split in two: Before Betsey and Since Betsey. When she died, I felt driven to write about the life of the woman who led me out of the slough of despond and provided the loving home I wanted and badly needed. I have written or coauthored a dozen or so books as well as a good many articles, essays, and reviews, but I do not know how I am supposed to limn Betsey. At her funeral, Monsignor Richard Lopez, our Father Confessor, preached that nothing mattered to her more than truth. He knew her well and read her right. She would be distressed if I embellished the story of her life, presenting her as unblemished, as a veritable saint, as a reembodiment of Our Holy Mother Mary.

Hence my quandary. If only to avoid the commission of blasphemy, I dare not think of Betsey as unblemished and saintly, much less as immaculately conceived. (I assume that these words are being read by people who—unlike most college professors and TV celebrities—do not confuse the Immaculate Conception of Mary with the Virgin Birth of Jesus.) But I do think of Betsey as a woman who graces the Kingdom of Heaven, and I trust that "all the angels and saints" appreciate the gift of her presence. If that identifies me as a doting old fool, so be it. I have been called much worse.

Shortly after Betsey died, I rummaged through the notes on southern history that we had accumulated over decades. I reread a letter from a powerful nineteenth-century politician from upcountry Georgia. I groaned. How I wished that I had been capable of writing such a letter to Betsey. In the Confederacy's dark days of 1864, General William Tecumseh Sherman devastated the world of Benjamin H. Hill. Beside himself, Hill wrote a letter to his wife, Caroline. In today's world of Beautiful People—dissipated Hollywood sophisticates, media philistines, and academic wannabes—Hill's letter would doubtless provoke guffaws and no end of clever witticisms. I nonetheless suspect that he articulated the innermost feelings of no few men, then and now, for the women they love.

You are so much better than I that I often feel humbled. In qualities that elevate and dignify; in virtues that are pure, sin-

3

cere, and steadfast, I never saw the equal of my wife. . . . I have
at least the very comforting reflection that it has ever been my
business to serve you, my delight to please you, and my ambi-
tion to be like you. . . . If to appreciate one's companion be the
virtue of domestic life, then this is my solid merit, for whether
I have a country or not, even a home or not, I expect to die as I
have lived—my wife's worshiper.

I recall my childhood and youth as grim and my early manhood
as distasteful. I committed sins, errors, and stupidities that, in retrospect, make me cringe, especially for people I hurt along the way.
Somewhere, I came across Benjamin Disraeli's thoughts in *Coningsby*
(1844): "Youth is a blunder; Manhood a struggle; Old Age a regret."
Let everyone speak for himself. Thanks to Betsey, most of my middle
age and my old age have been all I dared hope for. As for regrets, I
know of no more fruitless pursuit than "If I knew then what I know
now," or "How could I have been so stupid?" Or, "How could I have
made such a mess of my life?" If I had not lived as I had—for better or
worse, mostly worse—I probably would not have met Betsey. Inadver-
tently, I followed a winding and beclouded path to our first meeting.
I remain in awe of—and grateful for—the grace of God that made
possible the path and its terminus.

1

A Blind Date

You shall forget these things, toiling in the household
You shall remember them, droning by the fire,
When age and forgetfulness sweeten memory
Only like a dream that has often been told
And often has been changed in the telling. They will seem unreal.
Human kind cannot bear very much reality.

—T. S. Eliot, *Murder in the Cathedral*

Death Warmed Over

A married colleague in the Department of History at Sir George Williams University kept talking about the uncommonly bright and cultured twenty-seven year-old Elizabeth (Betsey) Fox, a teaching fellow at Harvard, who was writing a doctoral dissertation on eighteenth-century French History. My colleague had earned his Ph.D. at Cornell University under the direction of Professor Edward Whiting Fox, Betsey's father. He had known Betsey since her mid-teens and taught her at Cornell, where she spent a year between graduation from Concord Academy and matriculation at Bryn Mawr College. Occasionally reinforced by others, he went on and on about this princess. What was he thinking of? The last thing I needed in my erratic social life was a long-distance affair in Cambridge. One day he caught me in one of those maudlin moments that plague single men, however "macho" their strutting. "Enough! Give me her phone number. If she is half of what you keep advertising, she's worth a plane fare to Boston." I was hardly thinking of anything serious, but she seemed worth dallying with on occasional trips to professional meetings in Boston.

I called her, saying that our mutual friend had spoken highly of her; that I was going to Boston on business (a lie); and that I would welcome an opportunity to enjoy her company at dinner. The voice on the telephone was deep, cold, and forbidding. I almost hung up. But she did, if warily, assent to have dinner with me. Later I learned that her deep, cold, forbidding voice was not a patch on her mother's.

In Cambridge, I walked up a couple of flights to Betsey's apartment at the head of the stairs. Having expected a good-looking young woman, I came face to face with Death Warmed Over. She stood in the doorway, not slender, as I had been led to believe, but emaciated, yellowish green skin taut on her sunken face. I handed her a dozen long-stemmed roses. She thanked me warmly. That did not surprise me. I expected good manners from a properly reared *bourgeoise*. What did surprise me was her smile. How could Death Warmed Over have so breathtaking a smile?[1]

Still, Betsey's appearance jolted me: "What the devil did I get myself into?" As she poured me a drink in the kitchen, I reminded myself that I owed this young woman a pleasant evening. I made up my mind to do my best and to write the trip off as a bad bet.

---

1. As an old man remembering his youth, I offer a word of advice to young men. Civilized young women accept flowers graciously and with evident pleasure. The obnoxious pseudo-sophisticates who fill a modern Gomorrah like Manhattan are another matter. Expect a smirk and: "You have to be kidding?" Or: "Oh, haven't you heard? Chivalry is dead." Or: "Are you old-fashioned about everything else?" The last is a sure indication that you will prefer to end the evening with a cold shower.

There was good reason for Betsey's emaciation, taut skin, and unpleasant pallor. She was slowly recovering from hepatitis and anorexia, which in combination had almost killed her. People who knew her in her stressful years shook their heads at how bravely she had brought herself up short, sought the help she needed, and did everything necessary to save herself. Her close friend Nancy Wilson told me in later years that I had no idea of how sick and emaciated Betsey had been—that by the time I met her she had come back a long way. Before our marriage, as I got to know Betsey, I marveled at her strength of character—her steadiness, refusal to feel sorry for herself, will to pull herself together, and acceptance of responsibility for the anorexia. I made the mistake of saying so. She looked at me as if I had arrived from Mars: "You play the cards you're dealt." That may have been the only cliché she ever dropped on me, but, cliché or no, it remained her guiding star. She held fast to it throughout her life, although when she entered the Catholic Church in 1994, she referred to it as God's will. She wrote in her private notebook on October 25, 2002: "Devil distracts us—e.g., encourages us to blame others. Love for God helps us to overcome pulls of selfishness. Confession: not feeling guilty, but a courageous saying to God, Yes, it is my fault."

When I arrived at five p.m., Betsey looked terrible. At six or so, she wasn't all that bad. At seven she had become sort of nice-looking. By eight, sitting across a table at Restaurant le Maître Jacques, she had blossomed into lovely. When I left her at one a.m. with a kiss on her forehead, she was radiantly beautiful. Almost forty years later, she was in immeasurably worse shape than when I first laid eyes on her. Physically broken and fighting for life, she was unable to get out of bed by herself; barely able to walk; wracked by relentless, searing pain. Still radiantly beautiful.

We spent our first evening together talking history for hours, with a smattering of politics and an exchange of academic horror stories. I had never experienced anything like that evening. When I called her, I did not intend to spend an evening talking history. Quietly scintillating, she had an understated, entrancing, but never mean-spirited sense of humor. The extraordinary breadth and depth of her reading and culture took me aback. After all, she was a twenty-seven-year-old graduate student—a "kid." My knowledge of European history took her aback. Not many American historians of the United States know nearly as much European history as they should. Betsey and I had some good-natured exchanges over professional controversies. We quickly agreed that Eric Hobsbawm was a great historian. She was pleased to hear that I knew him and glowed when I offered to introduce her to him. She thought Georges Duby a greater medieval historian than Marc Bloc. I demurred. In later years she came to agree with me. At the time, I did not recognize that that would be one of the few such disputes with her I would ever win.

I inquired about her doctoral dissertation. She identified her subject as the Physiocrats—eighteenth-century pioneers in political economy. I took a long swig of gin. I had taught medieval and early modern political economy and knew much more about the Physiocrats than she was prepared for. "So, you think you have something to add to what Marx, Schumpeter, Weulersse, and the best recent scholars have said about the Physiocrats?" She replied without a moment's hesitation: "Yes." Not another word. I had asked her a question; she had given me an answer. Another long swig of gin and a thought: "Gene, you just met a big winner or a big loser."

Betsey, in her early twenties, had fallen in love with a Frenchman, but she ended their engagement when she reflected on what her life in Paris would be like. Thereafter, she had suitors in and around Harvard, including the rich and well-connected. She had no intention of following college friends in quick and tentative trips to the altar. Most of them divorced after a few years or lived in shaky marriages. She intended to marry once and spend her life with one man in sickness and in health, forsaking all others. She told her sister Rebecca and

8

June 6, 1969—Our wedding

Nancy Wilson—and told me later—that when she closed her door at one a.m. on our first date, she soberly and without a romantic rush said to herself: "Well, this is it. I just met the man I am going to marry." After two divorces, I proceeded cautiously, trying to rein myself in. But I knew that she had gotten to me.

Our blind date stretched into three days. I was due at Smith College the next day to keynote a conference on slavery in the Americas. I impulsively suggested that, as a historian, she might enjoy the scene. "If you find that I am not to your taste, don't worry. There will be a slew of scholars and writers, and I promise not to take it amiss if you latch on to someone else." Magnanimity? Not really. What did I have to lose? Some young lovelies usually attend these meetings, and I assumed that I would not lack for an appealing digression if Betsey looked elsewhere. As it happened, she did no latching. Several colleagues did, however, "hit" on her. Apparently, they saw her not as I had seen her at five p.m. on the previous day, but as I had seen her at one a.m. There are probably no men readier but less competent at approaching women at inappropriate times and places than college professors. Betsey, having been raised in academia, ran into them all her life. She thought them funny. I thought them less funny, but she brought me up short: "You have to understand, Gene, a great many professors, being little boys, are not quite housebroken."

As a girl, Betsey learned to accept responsibility and to persevere. When she first went to school in France, she plunged into subjects taught in French, a language she was just learning. She became flustered, particularly when she could not follow the instruction in mathematics. Learning math was hard enough, but in a language she was not at home with? Her teacher assured her that, if she worked hard, she would soon be soon be speaking good French and doing well in mathematics. She worked hard, played the cards dealt her, and proved him right.

Betsey learned valuable lessons from her struggle to overcome hepatitis and rescue herself from the anorexia she blamed on herself. Living on an even keel, she became an athletic coach's dream. Success, praise, and good fortune did not go to her head; reversals, bad breaks, and vicious attacks did not discourage or deter her. One way or the other, she slept soundly until her last years of acute physical pain. I teased that she would sleep through a nuclear war, and I was not far off. Her experiences help to explain her lifelong impatience with— not to say disdain for—people who whine and wallow in the cult of victimization. One of academia's self-dramatizers emoted: "I am triply oppressed—as an African-American, as a woman, and as a lesbian." Betsey had mastered the art of the poker face—she was, literally, a good poker player—but this time she failed. Casting her eyes upward, she fell silent. I only wish I could describe the look on her face.

Good and bad news in Betsey's kitchen: The first time Betsey invited me to dinner, she served a delicate fish. I seem to recall *sole meuniére*, or was it *truit amandine?* No matter. It was mouthwatering. When I was growing up, my Catholic family observed meatless Fridays. I enjoyed Friday dinner only on occasion, when my mother served hard-shell crabs or, even better, *scungilli* [conch] in a light, spicy tomato sauce. Usually, she fried breaded filet of flounder or something like it. It tasted like cardboard. I grew up hating fish. To my great pleasure, I relished Betsey's and have enjoyed fish ever since. A disagreeable turn followed her wonderful dinner. She asked me to get something from her kitchen cabinet. When I opened the cabinet door, I found cans or jars of spaghetti in tomato sauce. I did not believe that a woman who took such pains with complex French dishes would commit such an atrocity. Was I dating the daughter of Attila the Hun or some other barbarian? Should I report her to the Feds for what we would now call a hate crime against Italian-American culture? Apparently, she did not take Italian cooking seriously. I did my best to check myself, but it was not easy. It were as if she had spit in the holy water at St. Patrick's Cathedral or, worse, desecrated Lenin's tomb. I prepared to teach her the essentials of Italian cooking but quickly found that she knew all about them. She had just not cared. Betsey was nothing if not sensible. Having taken up with an Italian-American, she elected to mend her ways and apply herself. It did not take long for her to become a better Italian cook than my mother—and just about everyone else I knew.

Shortly after we met I learned just how madly Betsey had fallen in love with me. Apropos of nothing, she sent me a love letter. Tender, sweet, and simply written, it made my head swim. I had never received anything like it. She remarked in some detail how much she enjoyed dancing with me, depicting the movements of my shoulders and hips. Now, I had always been a poor dancer—real lousy. A boy in the age of the Lindy, I had to endure the ridicule of the Italian-American girls in my neighborhood for my physical clumsiness as well as my social ineptness. They made no secret of considering me a "drip"—in today's parlance, a "nerd." In later years, I tried to dance the Twist but looked and felt ridiculous. I welcomed the advent of freeform rock-and-roll dancing if only because I did not do much worse than many others. Yet Betsey meant every word. She loved to dance with me. Now, what else but the blinding passion of a lovesick young woman could account for her failure to notice that I had two left feet?[2]

---

2. You may wonder: What accounted for the metamorphosis of a "drip" into a perceived "lady's man"? It was easy. A man's reputation for appealing to lovely

Family Rumbles

Betsey's parents made clear that under no circumstances would they meet me, much less have me in their home. Having gotten an earful through the academic gossip mill, they raked her over the coals. When Betsey came to Montreal for a weekend, a professor at one of the local universities, who had known her father at Cornell, saw us on the street. People who lead unsatisfying lives need to distract themselves at other people's expense. In particular, a distressing percentage of college professors qualify as busybodies, gossips, and scandal-mongers. Apparently, this chap aspired to be world-class. He called Betsey's parents to tell them that he had seen her with—would you believe?—the politically notorious and womanizing Gene Genovese. Right out there in public, walking down Rue Sainte Catherine. As for my political notoriety, I became—improbably—the principal issue in New Jersey's 1965 gubernatorial election in the wake of a speech in support of the Communist revolution in Vietnam that I delivered at a teach-in at Rutgers University. Let me brag: So far as I know, I remained the only professor in America whom Richard Nixon personally and publicly campaigned to get fired. Thus, I had the fifteen minutes of fame that Andy Warhol assured us every American could have.

Betsey and I were having lunch when the phone rang. "May I speak to Betsey?" The deep and inhospitable telephone voice made Betsey's sound girlish. The voice did not identify itself but did not

---

women enormously inflates his appeal to women who ordinarily would not give him the time of day. To acquire such a reputation, remind yourself that you are not Rudolph Valentino, Clark Gable, Robert Redford, or whoever leads today's charts. Be sure to develop a thick skin when women reject you. Never let the rejections make you feel inadequate; retain a sense of humor; and proceed without rancor. People see you with a different lovely every six months. How can they know that you had approached a hundred women that year and that ninety-eight told you to get lost? You have to be dreadful not to appeal to 2 percent of the women you meet—in fact, 1 percent will do. There will always be one or two good-looking women who find a man attractive for qualities that most women find unexciting, off-putting, even abhorrent.

have to. I handed the telephone to Betsey: "It's your mother." Betsey gasped, "What? That can't be. She wouldn't do that." I repeated, "It's your mother." The brief conversation quickly turned rancorous. As I got up to leave the ladies to themselves, I heard Betsey say in a cutting tone: "You are wrong, mother. He used to have a girl in every city in North America."

Betsey was livid. I tried to cool her off. During our years together, I frequently lost my [Sicilian] temper at something or someone, and she quietly cooled me off with her [English] reserve. On this occasion we reversed roles. I saw no good in her opening a rift with her mother and father; even less did I want to do anything to widen a breach that might develop. It did not take me long to see that, notwithstanding inevitable tensions, she loved and honored them, and I took for granted that they loved her.

After the contretemps with mama, I questioned Betsey about her parents' attitude toward a man they had never met.

> Do your parents object to me because I am Italian-American?
>
> No. They are not bigots.
>
> Because I come from a working-class family?
>
> Not possible.
>
> Are they upset about my procommunist politics and current political notoriety?
>
> No, as anticommunist as they are, they are not Manichaean and do not confuse the political with the personal. Their old friends at Harvard include Frank Manuel, Paul Sweezy, F. O. Mathiessen, and others on the far Left, including Communists.
>
> Not my being Italian. Not my coming from the working class. Not my politics. In that case, let it be. They will accept me when they see that I am good for you. It will take time. Meanwhile, the source of their objection is clear enough, and I am not about to resent them for it.

[She got furious.] My parents brought me up to know my own mind and to make sensible choices. They ought to have confidence in my judgment of the man I have chosen to be with. Their attitude is insulting.

Well, okay, but I have to tell you: If I had a daughter in her twenties who was seeing a twice-divorced thirty-eight-year-old man with a reputation for promiscuity and troublemaking, I'd have him dealt with.

It ended well. Cornell's Department of History invited me to speak. To Betsey's surprise and mine, her parents called her to suggest that she come to Ithaca and invite me to stay at their home. I expected them to receive me courteously. They were, I knew, civilized people. Still, they received me with unexpected warmth, and we had a lovely time at dinner. (I suspect that they had checked me out in friendlier circles, but I never inquired.) We took to each other right away, and before long we became close friends. In time, Betty (Betsey's mama, the family's *grande dame*) came to think that I walked on water and tolerated not a negative word about me. I was relieved by, and grateful for, her affection. Recognizing her as a formidable woman, I did not want her for an enemy.

A Trip to Brooklyn

Months went by and I had not introduced Betsey to my family or even mentioned her to my father and brother. I was on the road a good deal, and in truth did not have much time to catch my breath. But there were other considerations. I was uneasy at the thought of bringing a third fiancée home to a traditional Catholic family and neighborhood. Among our people, only Protestants and other odd people divorced. I was thinking of ways to inform them that the family's black sheep was at it again. I loved and took pride in my family but had another concern. Alzheimer's disease struck my mother at sixty-five, and my aged father firmly assumed responsibility for taking care of her at home. He adamantly refused to have her committed: "She'll be dead in a year in one of those places." He took care of her for the next eleven years with the help of a part-time nurse. No, he did not necessarily do it out of love. I am not sure that my mother and father liked each other much. Husband and wife till death do us part. He performed heroically. It was nevertheless a deeply depressing scene, and I did not want to throw Betsey into it until I had had a chance to prepare her.

One day I returned to Montreal from a lecture tour to receive a call from Betsey. She bubbled about how much she enjoyed meeting my family. "What? How? What do you mean?" Where?" She had called my brother, who had not heard of her existence, and said that, since we planned to marry, it was time they met. Nancy Wilson and her husband, Peter, drove Betsey to the far end of Brooklyn, dropping her off in an Italian working-class neighborhood out toward Coney Island, sandwiched between Bensonhurst and Bay Ridge, not far from the aptly named Gravesend Bay, where the Mafia disposed of corpses wrapped in cement. Betsey fell in love with my family and my family with her.

Sometime in the 1970s a university in Manhattan approached Betsey about becoming dean of the liberal arts college. She had always thought she wanted to become president of a woman's college, and a college deanship would have been a stepping stone. But she slowly learned that she loved teaching too much to want to become an administrator. While she pondered her options, she worried about my reaction. We lived in Rochester, and I would have had to commute. I made clear that I would do so. (When in later years she moved to Emory University, I commuted from Atlanta for a number of years.) Betsey knew that I despise Manhattan and its trifling, self-inflated intellectuals, who utter incessant denunciations of elitism and bigotry while they personify what they denounce. I asked gingerly if she would consider living in my old neighborhood and arrange a limousine service for her daily commute to Manhattan. Elated, she did not hesitate. Although she did not despise Manhattan as I did, she said that she, too, preferred to live in my old neighborhood, which she had come to love. But she teased: "I thought that, as a boy, you hated your neighborhood and could not wait to get out of it?" So I had said; so I had long thought. Years among the Beautiful People of Chelsea, Greenwich Village, and uptown Manhattan, to say nothing of their epigone, in academia, called to mind Charles Dickens' observation: "One always begins to forgive a place as soon as it's left behind." Those words might be taken in mutually exclusive senses. For me they meant that I wanted to go home again.

Much as Betsey took to Sicilian-American ways, she and I had some ethnic difficulties. Like most Sicilian-Americans I have known—or other Italian-Americans for that matter—when something angers me, I raise my voice and gesticulate. Betsey shook when I raised my voice. She did not much like noise of any kind, and she found these displays threatening. "Why are you yelling at me? What did I do to make you so angry?" I had a great deal of trouble convincing her that, when I yelled, I was yelling at something or someone else, and that I never, never—hardly ever—yelled at her. Priding herself on being able to understand and appreciate Sicilian-American ways—not to mention understand her husband—she tried hard to accept my explanation, but it took her years to believe it. And I am not sure that she ever did so entirely.

Marriage

At Betsey's mama's "request," we were married at the Harvard Club of New York. I cannot say that I liked the idea. The Ivy League world was not my turf, and Betsey was less than enamored with the idea.

*June 5, 1969—
dinner party on
the eve or our
wedding*

But I was not about to irritate mama. Betsey wore a Pucci as her wedding dress. In the 1960s, Emilio Pucci made astonishing dresses, the colors of which defied belief. I bought Betsey a half-dozen, one more spectacular than the other. They were cut miniskirt—the vogue—and since her winsome figure sported lovely legs, the dresses were particularly flattering. Regrettably, Sr. Pucci subsequently exposed himself as perpetrator of a Crime against Humanity. He doubled the price (for which he might be forgiven) and drastically reduced the quality of his dresses (for which he should never be forgiven). Out went the glorious colors; in came dull and ordinary substitutes. I loved to see Betsey in the original Pucci dresses, but I would not have bought her one of the new ones at any price. With a touch of horror, I can imagine her look of displeasure and disillusionment if I had descended to such poor taste.

We had a fine, dignified ceremony conducted by a judge, after which our party settled in for dinner. I had a good-sized collection of rock-and-roll records: Beatles, Booker T. and the MGs, Four Tops, Supremes, Shirelles, Mamas and Papas, Jefferson Airplane, and others I no longer remember. The Harvard Club rocked, and the dancing went on for hours. The waiters and staff members were beside themselves: "Mister, thanks for a great evening. Take our word for it. This is a first for this place."

People close to Betsey knew that her poise and self-assurance obscured a genuinely modest assessment of her talents and accomplishments. Although she welcomed good words from others, she kept her priorities straight. She never took her press notices seriously. In her private notebook she took as her guide the words of St. Bernard: "Why am I so solicitous for the judgment of others or even our own when their opprobrium cannot condemn us nor their praise save us." Betsey, absorbing the sentiment, stood on every word, but, as it turned out, she did not perform flawlessly. Only on the rarest of occasions did she sink into self-deception, but she did think that she had some talents she did not have—notably, a good singing voice. I discovered the dismal truth when we started to attend Mass together. Still, unlike her husband, she could carry a tune. Much worse, a good many people will attest to her having been an extraordinary cook, but there were one or two matters in which she fell short. She boasted that she made excellent omelets, much better than her husband's. Emphatically, I deny it. She overcooked her omelets, whereas I cooked mine to perfection.

An even darker cloud hung over our marital harmony. Her *boeuf bourguignon, daube,* and beef stroganoff were glorious, but we did not eat beef often. We preferred hamburgers to steaks, except for an occasional filet mignon. Atlanta has a number of restaurants that make good hamburgers, the best of which we considered Roxx in our neighborhood. We had dinner there every other week or so. Warm and inviting, Roxx serves a variety of good food and has well-selected inexpensive wines. We almost always had a hamburger plate with excellent French-fries or tavern chips and a superior Caesar salad. A straight proprietor with a wife and children employs a mostly gay staff and has what appears to be a largely gay clientele. As in other restaurants we frequented, the staff seemed especially fond of Betsey. When her physical condition worsened, the waiters watched her like hawks, treated her gently, and showed her every kindness. Still, I had to wonder if our marriage could survive a public display of incompatibility. A sophisticated man of the world, I of course ordered my hamburgers rare. My wife ordered hers well-done. But then, she ate chicken and fish as well as meat well-done: "If it was ever alive, I want it dead, dead, dead." At home, she butterflied her own filet mignon, making sure that it showed no trace of pink. Dutiful wife that she was, she cooked mine precisely to my taste. Betsey had spent a good deal of time in Paris, and I wondered how Parisian restaurants endured her enormous lapse from good taste. I reminded myself that even Parisians are not entirely devoid of civility. For one thing, they will let an attractive woman get away with almost anything. After much prayer and reflection, I forgave Betsey for disgracing our family, and she expressed gratitude for my forbearance. At least that is how I interpreted her "Yes, dear."

Betsey had any number of idiosyncrasies. When I was a boy during the Great Depression of the 1930s, my mother would stock up on foodstuffs and household supplies during the summer months when my father, a dock worker, found work. The stored pasta, canned tomatoes, tomato paste, cooking oil, soups, and much else served us well during the winters when work on the docks was hard to find. Since my father refused to consider "relief," as welfare was then called, we had a rough time during a large part of the year. You would think that Betsey, too, had been a Depression baby by the way she stocked up. No matter how full the pantry and household closet, she insisted that you could never have enough "back-up." It worked reasonably well up to a point. We periodically donated our surplus of canned soups, pasta, and household supplies to our Church's collections for the poor. I am afraid, however, that we wasted a good many items, especially ingredients for the salads she enjoyed in great quantities. That hurt her. She did not like to throw things away. Her peculiarity had a redeeming consequence: Since she was an obsessive collector, the Southern Historical Collection at the University of North Carolina, which requested her voluminous personal and professional papers, has gotten more than it may have bargained for.

A more serious point of contention: Betsey and I loved to cook with garlic, and I used at least half a head in my *aglio/olio* pasta sauce with a touch of red pepper and fried slices of wafer-thin zucchini. I learned the recipe from my mother and do believe that it will earn both of us God's favor. Betsey much enjoyed it, but she had a complaint. Before I met her, I discarded the garlic as I poured the oil and zucchini over pasta. She objected. She enjoyed munching on fried garlic. She even asked that, instead of frying the garlic in whole cloves, I slice them finely and sauté them delicately so that she could get the fullest enjoyment. Choking, I protested her uncouth bourgeois WASP eating habits, which contrasted so crudely with my proletarian Sicilian fastidiousness at table. Meek and subservient to her husband's wishes, she yielded to my stern reprimand, restricting herself to a shyly worded petition for a slight adjustment. If I let her eat the garlic, she would compensate me. She would sleep in the guest room that night and refrain from kissing me goodnight. The human being truly has vast powers of adaptation. Suddenly, I learned to relish the smell and taste of garlic on her breath.

Other peculiarities: Betsey slept to my right at home—the side closer to the bathroom. She therefore insisted on sleeping to my right in hotels and everywhere else. When multiple sclerosis (MS) crippled her, I wanted her to sleep on the side of the bed closest to the hotel bathroom so as to reduce the chances of her stumbling during the night. I had a devil of a time overcoming her fanaticism. The change, after all, would interfere with her routine. She finally yielded with the greatest reluctance. And then, there was her demand that the Pellegrino bottles positioned in a semicircle in our refrigerator be removed from the left, never from the right. She had a flock of such little do's and don'ts, to which I adhered—if groaning. But one drove me crazy. She indulged it over and over again despite my entreaties and her promises to reform. My self-disciplined, well-organized wife could not remember to close the doors to the kitchen cabinets. Day after day I gently corrected her; day after day she apologized; day after day she repeated the transgression. At last, I decided to shame her. I said nothing further and closed the cabinet doors myself. I never doubted that my chivalry would fill her with guilt. And it might have, if she had noticed.

In view of Betsey's shortcomings, I had to consider whether I did not have the solemn duty to chastise her—to give her a beating for her own good. I told myself that the old patriarchal way remained the best and that moderate physical correction should be restored at law. I changed my mind—not because of some tedious treatise on women's rights, or the latest manifesto of rage against patriarchal oppression, or the foot-stamping of politically correct bores, or even the admonition of the Church. I changed my mind because I saw Betsey play softball. Her father had gotten her up at four or five a.m. to train her in softball, tennis, and much else. ("Oh, yes," she explained, "I am my father's first-born son.") Thirty years ago, women's athletics were far behind what they are now. Betsey was ahead of her times. She did not "throw like a girl"—that is, shot-put the ball. She threw overhand like a boy. She developed a strong and accurate arm and became a pretty good pitcher and first baseman. Much more important for immediate purposes, she could hit. She lacked long-distance power but sprayed hard line drives to all fields. She exercised daily and kept in shape. She may have looked frail—she did have frequent periods of poor health—but she was surprisingly strong. I have gone through life with the belief that an incompetent and sadistic medical profession has tried to impose exercise on us as part of a plot to annihilate people and curse the planet with underpopulation. And yet, sipping martinis as I observed Betsey's regimen, I gauged her physical strength. Hence, it occurred to me that if we ever got into a fight, she probably would deck me. Being a quick-witted fellow, I reassessed the theological, theoretical, and existential implications and ramifications and opted for the high ground of principle. I concluded that no gentleman would ever resort to wife-beating. It was immoral, revolting, and utterly inappropriate to civilized life.

As I hope I have made clear, I learned to my disgust that, unlike our Blessed Mother Mary, Betsey had not been conceived immaculately. Disillusionment came early in our marriage. On the Upper East Side of Manhattan one summer evening, she destroyed in one stroke my illusions about her propriety. We took a short walk along First Avenue to a favorite restaurant. A charming black barker at a strip joint did his effervescent best to entice us. He handed me a leaflet with a picture of a luscious, nude young woman and a legend: "If you think I'm something, come in and meet my friends." I stuck it in my pocket. After dinner we retraced our route, and the same barker was about to hand me the same leaflet. I waved the one I had, and we walked on. He called after us: "Hey mister, I don't blame you for not coming in. If I had a foxy chick like that on my arm, I wouldn't bother either." I expected Betsey to be annoyed, insulted, indeed outraged at this latest evidence of male insolence and coarseness, this gross denigration of women, this unconscionable manifestation of insensitivity and moral obtuseness. Instead, my proper, well-bred, reserved, puritanical wife beamed. She beamed! As I never before or after saw her beam. She looked as if she had just entered the Kingdom of Heaven.

In fairness, I must record that Betsey had one or two disillusioning moments of her own. Although she did not drink martinis, she graciously prepared a double for me every evening before dinner. I introduced her to Tanqueray gin and Noilly Pratt vermouth, the ingredients for a perfect martini. Sensitive husband that I was, I courteously congratulated her every day on a fine martini, cautiously suggesting that it might be a touch drier. Day after day she made the martini drier. Day after day, I congratulated her, suggesting that it might be a touch drier still. One day I sipped the martini and bathed her in kisses: "Betsey, you're wonderful, it's perfect." She did not take well to my gushing. Betsey almost never raised her voice, but raise it she did: "I knew it! I knew it! Of course I'm wonderful! Of course it's perfect! You're drinking straight gin."

Children

When Betsey accepted my proposal of marriage, she made clear that she wanted a large family. Soon to turn forty, I gulped: "Uh, how many children do you want?"

"A lot—about ten."

I quickly discerned that she was not kidding. "Uhhh, will you settle for four?" A bit put out, she grudgingly agreed to take it under advisement. Then she added:

> I hope you understand. I shall expect you to do a good deal to help raise the children, but I have no patience with this equal-parenting and quality-time nonsense. Children need a mother to be there for them if she possibly can. I know how strongly you want me to pursue an academic career, and I love you for your encouragement and support. But our children will come first. If I have to curtail my career or scuttle it altogether, that is what I shall do.

Not until Betsey entered the Church did she write much about her view of women's nature and place in the world. She had always believed in sexual equity, but, if I read her correctly, she considered sexual equality oxymoronic. I remember her spirited defense of women in the military: She scoffed at the notion that men and women could serve equally. She saw no need to deny that men were, in general, physically more capable than women for close-quarters combat. She therefore concluded that men should fill the infantry; and women, adjusting to their physical limitations, should run the war room and fly the attack helicopters, fighter planes, and bombers.

I admired Betsey's willingness to scuttle her career to devote herself to our children. Still, her remarks made me unhappy. She had extraordinary talent as a historian, and I fretted at seeing it go by the boards. But recognizing a *sine qua non* when I heard one, I was not about to challenge her. Betsey had a will of iron, although she did not flaunt it. In later years Monsignor Lopez dubbed her *Signora Testadura* (Madam Hardhead). Betsey subsequently added a postscript:

> Oh, one more thing. I do not intend to let you alone with our children until they are eighteen or so.
>
> What! What are you saying?
>
> You know as well as I do that you will be as unreasonably hard on your sons, as your father was on you. And you will let your innocent, precious, darling daughters wrap you around their fingers and get away with murder.

The story took an unforeseen turn. We tried to have a baby for a year or two but did not. Worrying about the possible effects of her earlier illnesses, Betsey feared that she might be barren. The doctors assured her that she was fine. Remembering that it takes two to make a baby, I had myself checked out. Bad news. There I was, married to a woman who wanted a passel of children and who would have been a marvelous mother. She loved children and, wherever we went in the following years, children adored her. How was I to break the news to her? She had driven me to the doctor's office and waited in the car. I got into the car unable to think of anything to soften the blow. I spit it out through clenched teeth: "I'm sterile." I held my breath as she stared out of the window for perhaps thirty seconds, which seemed an eternity. "Well, we'll have to reorient our life together." It came as no surprise that she said nothing hurtful at that moment. But I did wonder about the future: the cutting remark during a moment of tension; the penetrating silence at a difficult time; the unwelcome body language; the tears when she became depressed about losing her chance for motherhood. Women, like men, have ways of wounding those they love without saying anything directly, and muted messages are often the hardest to bear. I should not have worried. Never in all the years of our marriage did she hint at resentment—neither in word nor gesture nor deed. She simply closed the books, saying and doing nothing hurtful. More than once through the years she told people that her marriage—her husband—was the most important thing in her life. Her actions matched her words.

I deprived Betsey of more than the children she fervently wanted. Betsey loved to travel; I hated to. I accompanied her on one or two trips to Europe but resisted more than the essential minimum. She made some trips without me—to lecture abroad, to do research, to attend conferences, and to spend a term as a scholar-in-residence at the prestigious "*SciencePo*" (*Institut de Études Politique du Paris*). But she always kept them as short as possible.

That was not all. Shortly after we married she insisted—as she did every year thereafter—that we watch the Kentucky Derby on television. She could not contain her enthusiasm for the majestic horses. The only horses I recall having seen as a boy pulled pushcarts in Italian neighborhoods and the carriages at Central Park and the handsome but frightening police horses used to break up political demonstrations. When I married Betsey, I had never heard of the "horsy set" but asked if she had ever ridden. She acknowledged as much. I wondered if she would not like to go riding from time to time, saying I would gladly accompany her, if she wished, so long as she did not expect me to try to ride. She declined amiably, pleased that I had offered. We had a similar go-around about tennis, about which I knew and cared little. I knew that she had played a good deal when younger. I repeated the offer. Again, she declined. I rebuked her, calling her an "SSG" (a self-sacrificing girl) and asking what all this self-sacrifice was about. Despite her evasions, I knew what it was about. As the years passed, each of us took less and less pleasure in doing much of anything without the other.

Once in awhile we reversed roles, and she deprived me. Since my college years I have enjoyed Richard Wagner's operas, above all *The Ring Cycle*. When I made thirty dollars a week on the night job that paid my way through Brooklyn College, I spent more than I could afford at the Metropolitan Opera and fifteen dollars on Ernest Newman's splendid four-volume biography of Wagner. Betsey had a different view: She put up with Wagner's early Italianate operas, but loathed the rest, especially the *Ring Cycle*. She approved only of a few parts of—would you believe?—*Die Götterdämmerung*. I would have assumed that, if she found any part of the *Ring Cycle* sufferable, it would be from *Das Rheingold*. She could not bear *Das Rheingold*. Did I let her intimidate me? Certainly not. I stood up to her with full masculine dignity, asserting my rights and privileges as head of the family and master of the household. Scorning her irrational bias, I played *The Ring Cycle* whenever the spirit moved me. And the spirit did move me at times, notably, when she was out of town.

Married Life as "Struggle"

"Struggle" is a big word in the Wonderland of radical-chic intellectuals. Feminists and their fawning yes-boys trumpet the cant that "the personal is political"—a slogan that offers an excuse to mind everyone else's business and to impose your will. It has, by the way, largely gone unnoticed that the slogan derives from *La dottrina del fascismo* by Benito Mussolini and the Fascist philosopher Giovanni Gentile. But then Josef Stalin's *Mastering Bolshevism* will serve just as well.

It often seems as if the radical-chic intellectuals' greatest joy in life is "struggling" with—that is, abusing—other people, especially each other. At an organizational meeting to launch the journal *Marxist Perspectives* in the late 1970s, I made clear that I did not believe a committee-run journal could rise above mediocrity and that, as editor, I expected to retain full control of policy. If I did a poor job, the Publication Committee should replace me with someone to whom it ceded the same power. One of the sillier geese in our ranks looked put-upon: "But Gene, I want to be able to struggle with you." Afterwards, Betsey, who had an unerring eye for passive-aggressives as well as for dummies, enigmatically remarked to me, "I'll bet she wants to struggle with you."

Shortly after we moved to Atlanta, Betsey had lunch with a woman colleague. She returned home distraught. It took a great deal to make her distraught, and I asked what was wrong. She spoke with uncharacteristic rapidity, explaining that her colleague had complained angrily about the wretched behavior of her live-in. Betsey asked why she did not leave him. Her puzzled colleague maintained that such tension besets every "relationship." (Betsey and I despised the word and swore never to enter into a "relationship" with each other.) "After all, Betsey, it must be the same when you struggle with Gene." Betsey looked at me with disbelief. "Gene, you know how much I love you, and I know how much you love me. But if I had to struggle with you, it would not be worth it. I'd rather live alone. I waited to marry a man with whom I could share a life without serious domestic struggle. And I know you well enough to know that you couldn't tolerate it for long either." Having endured two dreadful, tension-ridden marriages, I assured her that she knew whereof she spoke.

Betsey believed that a woman who marries a man with the expectation of reforming him should have her head examined. She accepted me as a package and did not try to change anything of importance.

And yet, in numerous ways and without confrontation, she somehow changed me as no one ever had or could. Usually, I did not notice the effects of her indirect, not to say sly, methods. Let one example suffice. I did not much like the professorial option to dress "informally," which in practice usually meant sloppily; I always taught in three-piece suits. My impeccably dressed wife liked my three-piece suits but did not much like my wearing them to class. She once cautiously suggested that I might consider lightening up. I growled. That ended that. Then one day she bought me a birthday present—a light gray ultrasuede jacket. (I wonder why ultrasuede jackets disappeared after a decade. They were handsome, and I received many compliments on mine.) I was happy with my present and wore it to school for an occasional change of pace. She then gave me another, this time maroon, as an Easter present or something. Before long I had a half-dozen in different colors. I did not give up wearing my three-piece suits to school, but I did frequently vary them with ultrasuede jackets and, before long, other kinds of jackets as well. A Betsey performance. She did not like to argue with anyone, least of all with me. In all our years together she never nagged, harped, or harangued. She quietly placed tempting alternatives in her prey's sight and let nature take its course.

Her devious manipulation of her trusting, simple-minded husband knew no bounds. I watched movies with her on TV, but she rarely succeeded in dragging me to a movie theater. I can recall only about a half-dozen or so occasions during our marriage, two of which featured my old neighborhood in Brooklyn: *The French Connection* and *Saturday Night Fever*. When we moved to Ithaca, she was writing on fashion and wanted to see a film on the fashion industry. How could I refuse? The movie turned out to be *Dressed to Kill*. I like murder movies, so I found it just fine. But since it had nothing to do with the fashion industry, I rebuked her for deception. She pleaded not guilty, saying that she had no idea what the film was about and had been misled by the title. Maybe so, but since I was by no means sure,

I moved to get the upper hand. I announced that I forgave her since the movie contained a mouthwatering view of the gorgeous Angie Dickinson in the shower. I should have known better. Betsey lit up: She was so pleased that I had enjoyed the movie.

An incident may explain her attitude. One evening a beautiful young woman walked into the restaurant at which we were dining. All eyes turned, mine included. Embarrassed, I looked at Betsey, no doubt sheepishly. She flashed the wry smile she reserved for little boys caught with a hand in the cookie jar: "On the day a beautiful woman ceases to turn your head, I shall start to wonder if you are slipping into senility. By all means, enjoy yourself. Just keep in mind that an admiring look is one thing, a touch is another. Enjoy the one—in full knowledge that the other will cost you a loving wife."

Another cinematic moment said a good deal about the difference between Betsey and me. For many years we had a favorite movie, *Chariots of Fire*, which we saw once or twice a year, always finding something new in it. After we committed ourselves to the Church, we became curious about the hotly disputed *The Passion of the Christ*. Our respective reactions said more about each of us than I enjoy admitting. Our good friend Billy Hungeling joined us at a neighborhood showing on a Palm Sunday. As we left the theater, Betsey excused herself to go the ladies' room. Billy and I found *The Passion of the Christ* not merely powerful but shattering. We did not think we could sit through it again. Then Betsey, her face glowing, bounced up to us on her crutches: "Wasn't it magnificent? I can't wait to see it again." Billy and I looked at each other shamefaced, nodded, and grunted something or other.

Betsey and I talked little about our daily life together. We had no definite rules about respective duties and responsibilities and did not think of negotiating. I cannot imagine circumstances in which either of us would have considered living like that. But I may be off a bit. We articulated no rules because we shared a common understanding of do's and don'ts, which our respective parents—different as they were in ethnicity, class, education, and religion—brought us up on. Betsey's father (a learned and urbane intellectual) and my father (an uneducated but incredibly smart dock worker) took to each other right away; two strong men recognized a kindred spirit. In any case, Betsey and I proceeded without discussion. We always gave young friends unsolicited advice when they married: "Courtesy is the first rule of marriage." We both believed that when you stop saying, "excuse me," "please," "may I," "thank you," and "you're welcome," you have taken the first steps toward divorce. But those little courtesies have to flow easily. If they flow with the slightest touch of routine or boredom, you may as well not bother.

A "don't" went along with that "do." Father Richard Morrow delivered a sermon on marital quarrels at Atlanta's Cathedral of Christ the King. He told of hearing confession from a chap who was furious with his wife for her insufferable displays of resentment and anger. Father Morrow did his best to counsel patience and kindness, but the chap responded: "You don't understand, Father, I can take almost anything she dishes out except her constantly getting historical." Father Morrow corrected him: "You mean hysterical." "No, Father, historical. Every time we quarrel over something, no matter how trivial, she gets historical: 'Have you forgotten when you. . . . ?' 'Don't you remember that rotten thing you did when you. . . . ?' 'I'll never forget the time that you . . .'" Along with the rest of the congregation, Betsey and I enjoyed the story, but we did not need to hear the message. Neither Betsey nor I ever got historical. When we quarreled, we settled the issue within hours and left it there. I do not recall our carrying a quarrel into the next morning, much less dredging it up at a later date.

The subject reminds me of a few words of advice I received at age nineteen from Irving Feder, a friend at Brooklyn College and ever since. As usual, I was having a bad time socially. Feeling sorry for myself, I wailed that I needed a girl I could talk to. Only two years older than I but a good deal more mature and worldly, Irv snapped: "Gene, you don't need a girl you can talk to. You need a girl you don't have to talk to." He was right, but it took almost twenty years and a good many blunders to find her.

One day Betsey paid me the most loving of compliments. Her regular mammogram looked threatening. A second came back negative, but we had some bad moments in between. I was frightened that she might have cancer, but also that she might become disconsolate at losing one or both of her breasts. I begged her to get the safest treatment possible and not turn herself inside out if she needed a mastectomy. I had heard of men who became disoriented and could not adjust, of traumatized wives, and of marriages that buckled. Clumsily, I tried to assure her that she need not give such considerations a minute's thought . . . that nothing would ever shake us . . . that . . . that . . . She replied softly: "Gene, I'm not in the least worried about you and our marriage. Not for a minute in the years we've been together have I doubted that you would be there for me, no matter what."

Then, with that melting smile of hers, she alluded to her small breasts: "Let's face it. I don't have enough to make a fuss over anyway. And besides, I had the good sense to fall in love with an 'A' rather than a 'T' man."

2

A Soufflé

. . . having each other make[s] more of them both.

—Gail Godwin, *Evensong*

Betsey and I team-taught college courses, coauthored books and articles, and shared platforms at professional meetings. Colleagues often asked how we managed to work so closely without straining our marriage. We replied that spousal collaboration falls into the category the French invoke for making a soufflé: It is easy or impossible.

There are married historians who seem to collaborate splendidly—Professors William and Jane Pease come immediately to mind—but the list is short. A number of colleagues have admitted that an attempt to write or teach together would put their marriages at risk. Differences in temperaments, accommodated in most situations, can prove fatal in professional collaboration. If husband and wife cannot help competing with each other, if either party feels the slightest envy or resentment at the other's accomplishments, if each cannot genuinely enjoy every success scored by the other, then any attempt at professional collaboration invites serious trouble. Betsey, in her book *Feminism without Illusions: A Critique of Individualism* (1991), told how she regularly beat me at gin rummy and how, one day in a fit of frustration, I roared, "Fine, you beat me at gin rummy, but I have a penis, and you don't." With mortification, I confess that she told a true story. But women are conniving creatures. She failed to mention that I beat her at chess and that, in consequence, she stopped playing chess with me. With gin rummy, chess, and the NFL football pool in which we participated separately with several others—she usually won—we competed fiercely and without quarter: war to the knife, knife to the hilt. But those were the only things over which we competed.

Betsey and I began by teaching courses together at the University of Rochester. As in most universities, a two-semester course on Western Civilization was fast becoming a relic. It had long been required, serving as a prerequisite for history and other courses in the Humanities. It remains difficult to understand how anyone with a pretense at having an education can do without it. A new generation of ideologically motivated educators put an end to the requirement, denouncing it for Eurocentrism or some other hate crime. At Rochester, our course shrank to twenty-five or thirty students, although taught by a superior senior professor with a well-earned reputation as a fine teacher. Betsey had just joined the faculty as a lowly assistant professor. She coolly asked the chairman of the department (me) to let her teach it. Well, what did I have to lose? Among other advantages, she was the daughter and academic protégé of one of the greatest teachers of Western Civilization in the country. She put a hundred students in the classroom and doubled that number the following year, maintaining a high standard in grading. As the pressure on her mounted, we elected to team-teach the course. It was her course: She redesigned it with an unusual system of sections. The course met three times a week, twice to hear lectures, once in small sections. But the sections were not primarily for review and clarification of the lectures and reading assignments. Rather, she let each teaching assistant run the section as a mini-seminar devoted to a special subject: e.g., political history, political theory, economic development, religion—whatever the TA specialized in. The students signed up for the subject they found most attractive. She met with her TAs often, providing direction and encouraging exchanges of experience but not interfering unduly. A word of advice: Before you try it, make sure that you have first-rate TAs.

In our team-teaching in the early 1970s, there was no confusion of authority. For the most part, Betsey assigned the lectures I would deliver; in effect, I served as her assistant lecturer. I advised her only when she asked for advice—which was not often since she did not need much. I was grateful to her for allowing me to participate in teaching the course. Western Civilization had always been my favorite undergraduate course but, because of other responsibilities, I had not been able to teach it in years. When we subsequently team-taught a course on Marxism, we reversed roles. I served as the principal instructor. She deferred to me, as I had deferred to her in the course in Western Civilization. There were no difficulties in either course. We never discussed a pecking order. We never had to.

Betsey taught me something about a matter that had never been my strength—communication. I had a reputation as a good lecturer, but, having heard good and even great lecturers, I rated myself a "B." The first time I heard Betsey lecture in Western Civilization I hardly knew what to think. I found her dull. That she eschewed theatrics neither surprised nor bothered me. But she hardly gestured, rarely moved away from the podium, and restricted her humor to a few subtle asides. How did she manage to increase enrollments dramatically with a style like that? I noticed something. Even at my best, I always put some students to sleep. In Betsey's class I saw no nodding heads. The students listened carefully and busily took notes. She taught history as a narrative—a story. Her lectures were interpretative and analytical without appearing so. Interpretations and analyses flowed through the narrative, free of the affected pseudotheorizing and ideological crotchets that have become standard in college history courses as taught by mediocrities. She unostentatiously imparted and interpreted information at a pace that eased its assimilation. I may have thought her lectures dull; her students clearly thought differently. I frequently rediscovered that she had platform talents I lacked or could not match. Every couple of years or so during the 1990s, we both lectured at the Buckley School of Public Speaking in Camden, South Carolina. I hope I did a good job for our friend Reid Buckley and his school, but I do not need to be told that my performances never equaled hers.

In both courses at the University of Rochester there was an amusing side issue. When students had a problem, they almost invariably went to see Betsey, not me. Betsey had a reputation for listening and caring. I had a reputation for being unsympathetic and gruff. The result: The few students who came to me got the tongue-lashing they expected but often the concession they wanted. Those who went to Betsey found a kind, sympathetic, caring woman, but rarely, if ever, got what they wanted. She respected her students and patiently explained her reasons for proceeding as she did. As I knew from personal experience, she had the gentlest way of saying "No."

Once in a long while an awkward moment intruded on our professional collaboration. In 1983, we published *Fruits of Merchant Capital: Slavery and Bourgeois Property in the Rise and Expansion of Capitalism.* I had been seriously ill, and Betsey wound up doing two-thirds of the work. One of the chapters that I drafted contained a sentence we both modestly thought splendid and congratulated ourselves on: "Gene, that is one of the finest sentences you have ever written." Puz-

36

zled, I replied: "No, no, Betsey, I drafted that chapter, but you added that particular sentence. It is finely crafted, but by you, not me." She got her back up. We both knew that she had a much better memory than I. And, in her view, that settled the matter. She knew that I had written it. With equal certainty, I knew that she had. To the day she died each of us remained certain that the other had written it.

When we coauthored a piece, how did we reconcile disagreements? I would love to announce that we never disagreed, but I must admit that her wrong-headedness and obstinacy occasionally led her to question my infallibility. I learned on our first date that we shared principles and points of view, disagreeing about little. But what happened when we did disagree about the interpretation of data? If we could not settle the matter in an initial discussion, we knew something was wrong. We then went back to the sources, read them together, and exchanged versions of their meaning. Usually, it did not take long to arrive at a common judgment. In a few cases we recognized irreconcilable interpretations that we had to bypass in our joint publications.

At the beginning of our marriage Betsey was Elizabeth Fox Genovese. She said simply that she was proud to be Mrs. (and then Ms.) Genovese. So what accounted for the hyphen? Feminist ideology? Peer group pressure? No. Betsey did not give in to fads and pretense. After she joined the faculty of the University of Rochester she changed her name because the computer did not know what to do with us. It had trouble sorting out E. F. Genovese and E. D. Genovese. When students tried to enroll in my courses, they often found themselves in Betsey's—and vice versa. We took it lightly and lived with the inconvenience. But when the computer messed up our financial records, our forbearance disappeared. Betsey became Elizabeth Fox-Genovese and made her professional reputation under that name. Shortly thereafter I left the chairmanship of the department and gave up my telephone line. College policy required that, other than a department chairman, two professors had to share one line. So Betsey and I shared. Her line was always ringing, and when she was not in her office, I took the calls for her. Her callers, hearing me identify myself as her husband, addressed me as "Mr. Fox-Genovese"; increasingly over the years, mail arrived for Eugene Fox-Genovese. And it got worse. People inside and outside the academic world assumed that I was Mr. Fox-Genovese. To this day, much of my mail comes addressed to Eugene Fox Genovese (with or without the hyphen). I had prepared myself early. Shortly after our marriage, I suggested to her father—an accomplished and widely respected scholar and teacher—that within a decade or so Betsey would be *the* Fox and *the* Genovese in the historical profession. We could resent it or enjoy it. After grave deliberations we arrived at a difficult decision: We would enjoy it.

Temperament: Political and Other

Betsey brought me up short on my grand illusions, not to say pretensions. Something or other in the newspapers threw me into a fit—it happened often—and I announced to Betsey that I wished I had not been born in the twentieth century, which she knew I detested.

Oh? Well, what century would you have preferred?

The thirteenth! [Catholic traditionalists call it "the greatest of centuries."]

Gene, if you had been born in the thirteenth century, you would have been a serf on a feudal estate in Sicily. I do not think you would have enjoyed it.

Nonsense. I would have become a priest and risen to be a bishop, an archbishop, a cardinal, maybe even pope. [I always took a shy and retiring view of my abilities and prospects.]

The Church would doubtless have welcomed you into the priesthood and assigned you to a rural or small-town parish out-

38

side Palermo or Messina. And there you would have remained. You might have risen to be a pastor, but in case you have forgotten, the Church recruited its hierarchy from the upper classes.

Well, the Church made a serious mistake.

Maybe so, but that's not the question we are discussing.

Betsey and I shared political principles but not always strategy and tactics. Without shrinking, she made tough decisions when necessary, but she had the temperament of a moderate. In contrast, I never completely lost the shoot-from-the-hip temperament that led me to Stalinism in my teens. The first time we heard anything of importance about Boris Yeltsin, the mayor of Moscow, was a front-page story of his performance at a meeting of the Central Committee of the Soviet Communist Party. Yeltsin's speech criticized Mikhail Gorbachev and other party leaders for lagging in promised reforms. He spoke in a manner that violated Communist Party discipline and threatened to unleash an intraparty civil war. Betsey wondered what he was thinking. In her first book, *Origins of Physiocracy: Economic Revolution and Social Change in Eighteenth-Century France* (1976), she explained how the Physiocrats believed that those who wished to create a market economy needed political centralization—that the reforms necessary to build a market economy required what the Physiocrats called "legal despotism." Betsey had a firm commitment to democracy and hostility to despotism, but she also had a firm grasp on reality. Reviewing the upheavals in the Soviet Union, she doubted that Gorbachev could reform the economy without tightening the political regime to control rampant corruption, economic chaos, political strife, and veritable anarchy. Yeltsin's course worried Betsey; it infuriated me:

> Betsey, if Gorbachev is going to save the party, the Soviet Union, and the cause of socialism, he had better put down

these loudmouthed radical demagogues. They will wreck the party and render it incapable of mastering the crisis.

What would you do in Gorbachev's place?

Shoot the SOB.

Somehow, I thought you'd say that. I don't think it's a good idea.

Betsey, listen to me. I know Yeltsin's type. The Communist Party and the Left have always been full of ultra-radical criminals and fools—the fools more dangerous than the criminals. As you know, Lenin considered them infected by an "infantile disorder." If you do not deal with them . . .

Please forgive me for interrupting you, but your penchant for resolving crises by *coups de main* leaves something to be desired. Gorbachev came to power as a reformer who promised to open Soviet society to vigorous public debate, to lower the level of violence—in a word, to civilize a political system that you yourself call barbarous. He cannot possibly achieve those objectives without international support and goodwill—which he will forfeit if he shoots Yeltsin.

You just don't like to shoot people.

No, I don't, but that is not the point. Your preferred policy can't work, and you know it. So stop venting.

In the early 1990s at West Point, Betsey delivered one of her more impressive lectures, which came within a year of my lecture at Annapolis. Both of us spent time on campus, meeting students and participating in classes. We were enormously impressed by the quality of the instruction and by the acute intelligence and excellent preparation of the students. When we compared notes, we praised the obvious success of the services in instilling democratic values in their cadets and midshipmen. In particular the officers were doing a fine job of teaching in-depth the sorry record of the incompetence of military regimes around the world and of the necessity for military submission to civilian authority. Politically temperate, a reassured Betsey sighed with pleasure that America did not have a *coup d'état* military, but she seemed disconcerted when her husband—it was the Clinton years—looked depressed and wistful.

Consigliere

Once in a while Betsey's selected moderation—she called it prudence—saved my skin. Betsey and I tried, and generally succeeded, in not interfering in each other's professional affairs. We would use each other as sounding boards for possibly risky actions. Even then, the one advised the other in full knowledge that the advice might be rejected and that the rejection provided no occasion for resentment. No quarrels ensued.

Only twice did she forcefully intervene. During the early 1970s, when I was chairman of the Department of History at the University of Rochester, a close friend and colleague was going through a midlife crisis. Every year or so department chairmen have to hold the hand of one colleague or another who is coming apart. Chairmen have to be baby sitters to adults—a role I was not cut out for. My colleague insisted that the college owed him a leave. Kenneth Clark, the dean, refused to authorize it. Clark was the best dean I ever worked for. Shrewd, wily, and strong, he was no man to cross. With my colleague in a pet, I planned to help him out indirectly by not assigning courses to him for a semester. I prepared to send Clark the teaching schedule for the coming semester with my colleague free of teaching, although not technically on leave. Pleased by my own cleverness, I mentioned my intentions to Betsey. She raised her eyebrows, betraying a certain alarm. She said nothing but went to the departmental secretary, telling her to hold up my letter. She assured the secretary that she would accept full responsibility. The wary secretary predicted that I would have both of them killed. Before I could confront Betsey, she apologized for her intrusion. Sort of. "You know that Ken is no man to trifle with. As much as he admires you, he will take your head." I admitted that I knew she was right and, in truth, I was relieved rather than angry. But I fretted over having to deal with my colleague roughly, knowing that he was in bad shape and might do something stupid.

Betsey chided me for wandering too far from my Sicilian-American roots. "Please remember, that in your people's culture, the family never hands a miscreant over to *stranieri* [outsiders]. But when his behavior threatens the family, then the family itself deals with him." She pulled out a copy of Mario Puzo's *The Godfather*. I told her that, although I much admired Puzo's *The Fortunate Pilgrim*—a superior novel of Italian life in New York—I did not have time for or interest in Mafia novels. As usual, she did not argue. She opened *The Godfather* and read aloud a number of scenes. She began with one of her favorites, which she knew would get my attention: "Accidents don't happen to people who take accidents personally." Another had direct relevance. Don Vito Corleone explains the ways of the world to his son: "Michael, there are people in this world who go through life provoking dangerous men, when they themselves are without resources. You must have noticed them." I took the book and spent the night on the couch reading it. I went to see my colleague the next day to explain that, much as I loved him, I would "shorten him by a head" if he did not get a grip on himself. (The phrase came from J. V. Stalin, a boyhood political hero of his and mine.) Fortunately, he got the message.

Betsey joined our department in 1974, and my actions as chairman of the department had a direct impact on her for several years before she finished her dissertation and joined the faculty as an assistant professor. The administration brought me to the University of Rochester to clean up a mess. The department chewed up its chairmen, and I found myself the sixth chairman in six years. Among other niceties, the left-wing clique that constituted the department's oligarchy had never so much as interviewed a woman or a black for a faculty position. I arrived to find myself presiding over an all-male, lily-white department. The oligarchs paid themselves twice as much as they paid a fine full professor who refused to cotton to them; they hired assistant professors at twenty percent or so less than they were authorized to, thereby having funds to beef up their own shares; and they treated the graduate students so dishonestly that they went on strike—the only TA strike in the history of the university. I think I have a good sense of humor, but, somehow, I did not find any of it funny. I put an end to those abuses and, for my pains, acquired a reputation for ruthlessness—for being a pocket Stalin. I may well have qualified, but I would have been a lot more ruthless if Betsey had not counseled restraint. I listened to her, but on this matter, I wished I had not.

During my second year as chairman, five full professors, who envisioned themselves indispensable, demanded my resignation and threatened to resign from the University *en bloc*. It seems that I would not dare to force the resignations of the top five professors in the department. When I told Betsey, she burst out laughing: "Well, you had better get busy and recruit five new full professors." They then called on the administration to depose me. President W. Allen Wallis, like Clark, did not shrink from conflict, much less cave under pressure. But the department's poisonous atmosphere was wearing me down. Betsey to the rescue. She lectured me—something she had never done. As best as I can recall this was her unusually blunt speech:

> Your opponents have no principles, courage, or political competence. They care only for their salaries, perquisites, and academic baubles. They will never get the better of you unless your will falters, and letting your will falter is not your style.

Do nothing. Say nothing. Let them stew. They have no staying power. They will snivel, whine, throw tantrums, and accomplish nothing. Besides, they disrespect, dislike, and distrust each other and will not hang together long if you keep the pressure on.

I took her advice. The rebellion, incapable of producing a bang, petered out with a whimper.

Political Doings

My politically inexperienced wife had an irritating tendency to contradict me on political matters about which she knew nothing. Two illustrations will suffice. When we got the first inklings of the Watergate scandal, she asked me what I thought. I replied that it would turn out to be a tempest in a teapot and blow over with Nixon's re-election. We agreed that with an opponent like George McGovern, Nixon would not even have to campaign to win big. We both skipped the 1972 election, or rather forgot to take out absentee ballots when we moved to California for the year. Reviewing the accomplishments of Nixon's administration—effecting détente with the Soviet Union, recognizing Communist China, edging toward withdrawal from Indochina, and applying stopgap wage and price controls during a recession—we thought that on balance he had performed about as well as we might have hoped for from a left-wing President. Notwithstanding his impressive record and our poor opinion of McGovern, as leftists we could not have brought ourselves to vote for Nixon. Betsey nevertheless shook her head at my cavalier dismissal of Watergate. She thought the scandal would turn out to be a nation-shaking event and wreck Nixon's administration. She simply could not believe that the American people would tolerate it. I smiled at my wife's naiveté and dismissed Watergate as a pimple on the posterior of progress. Ingénue that she was, she held her ground with a "We'll see."

44

Years later, when William Jefferson Clinton disgraced the presidency and faced a growing political barrage, Betsey became alarmed. "Gene, he's going to commit one or another foreign-policy atrocity to cover himself. He's capable of anything, including provoking a war." Her politically sophisticated husband assured her that those days were over and that, in any case, Clinton could never get away with so transparently cynical a gambit. A few days later, Clinton attacked Afghanistan, with justification, and Sudan, with nary a shred. American politicians rushed to congratulate him on what, in the Sudan, qualified as nothing short of a major war crime that "the international community" has yet to investigate. I choked. Betsey shrugged: "What did you expect?"

Not until the end of the 1970s—when we launched the journal *Marxist Perspectives*—did I learn that Betsey had an astute political head. As editor, I intended to appoint a well-known Ivy League historian, a red-diaper baby, as "International Affairs Editor." The position was crucial. We had close relations with the Western European "Eurocommunists," notably the Italian Communist Party (PCI). I had no doubt that the success or failure of our journal—its prospects for becoming a serious contributor to American intellectual and political life—depended on the fortunes of Eurocommunism. And so it turned out.

When I told our comrades in the PCI of my first choice, they went cold. "Do you trust him and the others around you?" With undisguised annoyance, I replied, "Of course not, but I have to work with what I have." Their main man replied, "It is your choice, but, with all respect, comrade, we are wary of those people. If you send one of them to Rome, we shall receive him cordially but give him nothing we need to keep confidential." I winced: "It is precisely your confidential reports on world affairs that I need. So, just whom among my comrades would you trust?" They answered, "Your wife. If you send her, we shall provide her with confidential information for her and your eyes and ears only." I protested her lack of experience. She had never been active in radical movements, and although she was widely read and knew more about international politics than most of those in our circle, it was not her strongest suit. The reply, as best I can render their cautious language: "We know enough about her. She is acutely intelligent, learns fast, has excellent judgment, and is discreet." Betsey read Italian with ease, understood spoken Italian, and spoke it just well enough for business. She made a number of trips to Rome as well as Paris, and our Italian comrades kept their promise. They gave her invaluable detailed information on current events. And there were no leaks. Our Italian comrades treated me with respect, and I had evidence that they trusted me—up to a point. It was clear that a reputation for occasional rashness preceded me, as did her reputation for being able to check my indiscretions.

In Rome we had a brief meeting with Giorgio Napolitano, the PCI's man behind the throne, who at this writing sits as president of Italy. An impressive, unostentatious man, he was pleased that we were going to Bologna for a few days. He picked up the telephone and called Renato Zangheri, the Communist mayor of Bologna. Napolitano told him to expect a couple of American comrades and asked that he receive them well. When we arrived at our hotel, the staff was atwitter. You would have thought that the president and first lady of the United States had arrived. The staff had a message for us. Mayor Zangheri had left word that we should join him for dinner at the Ristorante Dante. Betsey called to explain that we had already had dinner. Zangheri asked that we join him anyway for dessert and coffee and a glass of wine. When we arrived, we found a table of about a dozen to fifteen people, mostly young. There were one or two political or administrative chaps; the rest were graduate students. After the amenities, I tried to direct the conversation to politics—discreetly, I hope. After all, presumably, the table was full of Communists. Naturally, I assumed that I, not my subordinate International Affairs Editor, was top dog. Besides, what else would they want to talk about except politics? It did not take me long to discern that I rated primarily as Elizabeth Fox-Genovese's husband. Zangheri politely made some brief chitchat but quickly made clear that we would have plenty of time to talk politics in the next few days. At the moment, he had more important matters in mind. Zangheri doubled as a professor of early modern history at the prestigious L'Università di Bologna and, like Betsey, was a specialist on the Physiocrats. He had invited Betsey to meet his graduate students. He much admired *Origins of Physiocracy,* assigned it to his seminar students, and wanted them to meet and engage her. It was quite a scene. Some of the students spoke English, more or less. Most spoke French but not all spoke well. Betsey cheerfully went back and forth in French, Italian, and English, translating for her dullwitted husband as she went along.

The Italians were like no Communists I ever met. Unusual for Communists, they had a rich sense of humor. They were courteous and gracious, and, however committed to their cause, they did not spew absurdities. Betsey and I long recalled a few incidents. But, first, I must pay tribute to the way they ran Bologna. The working-class housing overwhelmed us, standing in stark contrast to the quasi-slums that the Labor Party had, to our disgust, built in Britain. The policies introduced by the Communists encouraged tenants to buy their apartments and organize block committees to set rules in accordance with the wishes of tenants and owners. Now, Communists had always condemned such policies as reactionary *"Proudhonisme"* ever since Friedrich Engels published his book *The Housing Question.* We inquired into this local heresy: "Comrade Engels would not have approved." The reply: *"È morte il compagno Engels."* (Comrade Engels is dead.) The chief of housing looked puzzled: "Surely, comrades, you know that all experience shows that people without a personal stake in property will not take care of it." Margaret Thatcher, the rising star of British politics, must have enjoyed their policies, some of which were strikingly similar to those she subsequently introduced as prime minister. Betsey particularly wanted to know about the facilities for women and old people. No Potemkin Village tourist, she was not easy to fool. She gave the party high marks for what it was accomplishing under stringent financial restraints.

We had been told that Bologna had the best cuisine in the world. When we got there, we found it even better than advertised. I reveled in how good it was, but, then, I was no world traveler. Even my well-traveled Francophile wife, who knew Paris well, rejoiced at Bologna's cuisine. She complimented Zangheri on the food. "Yes," he replied, "even we [Communists] have not been able to ruin it." Then I committed a gaffe—"a Genoveseism," as called at home. Having noticed a small, centuries-old Chinese community in Bologna, I made the ghastly mistake of asking Zangheri how the Chinese voted. The words were hardly out of my mouth when Betsey turned white. She had carefully observed Zangheri's quasi-aristocratic style—a style she knew well from personal experience in Europe. Her look signaled that I had committed a *faux pas*. Zangheri, who has exquisite manners and indeed carries himself with aristocratic bearing, went cold. He stared at his plate of tortellini. We had been speaking English, but he replied to me in Italian: "*Sono cittadini di Bologna.*" (They are citizens of Bologna). Ouch. He was telling me, with little attempt to hide his irritation, that Communists, like other citizens of Bologna, valued each other more for contributions to their beloved city than for party affiliations.

My (More or Less) Faithful Translator

Not every part of my collaboration with Betsey was a joy. On one occasion I considered killing her. We were living in London during the academic year 1976–77 and about to fly to Italy for meetings with PCI comrades. I was groaning over my inability to speak Italian decently.

I read Italian adequately but had trouble understanding what was said to me and in speaking coherently once I got beyond a couple of sentences. I have what the Italians call "Restaurant and Bedroom Italian." Betsey piped up: "Don't worry, I'll translate for you." I knew she read Italian well but had no idea she could speak it. And she barely could. She nonetheless cheerfully assured me that she was boning up and would do fine after a couple of days. And so she did. Her accent left a good deal to be desired, but she understood everything said to her and replied in an Italian acceptable for all its being riddled with bits of French, Spanish, and English. In Bologna, Zangheri provided us with an interpreter. After an hour or so, the interpreter told Betsey that he was enjoying the day and would remain with us. But he assured her that she did not need his services as a translator, and that he would limit himself to correcting an occasional mistake. In Rome and Florence the story was the same. My half-WASP, half German-Jewish wife served as my translator. Embarrassed and humiliated, I looked out of our hotel window and thought about defenestrating her.

I knew enough Italian to keep her honest. French was another matter. I read professional work in French, Spanish, and Portuguese but could not speak a word, except for a little high-school Spanish. In Paris we saw a good deal of Albert ("Marius") Soboul, the Communist historian who held the chair in the French Revolution at the Sorbonne. He invited us to speak to his *colloque* on the colonial question in the French Revolution, particularly on the revolution in Saint Domingue (later, Haiti). There were several dozen people present, a majority of whom knew English. Betsey spoke first in French. I then spoke in English. Betsey translated step by step. We had long disagreed on one important matter, and I phrased my point of view carefully, but she translated me as saying something in accord with her own view. My spoken French may be virtually nonexistent, but I understood just enough. "Betsey, I didn't say that!" The English-speakers in the room roared. They understood what she had done—and she knew that they had understood. "No," she replied in her most charming manner, "but it is what you should have said."

She partly atoned at dinner that night. *Liberté! Egalité! Fraternité!* Soboul fumed that the French talked too much about liberty and not nearly enough about equality. An accomplished and intellectually serious historian, he thereupon delivered an extended exposition on the glories of equality—a shibboleth that I had never fallen for even in my hard-left days. Soboul spoke in French, but I gave Betsey no time to give me an English précis. I had struggled, with some success, to follow his French and replied on point in English. Betsey translated my words into French for him and other guests, this time precisely. But then, this time she agreed with much that I said. Soboul was not amused. Recalling the exchange in his *colloque* and annoyed at my intervention in response to a language I was supposed to be ignorant of, Soboul stewed: "You told me that your husband read French but could not speak or understand spoken French." Betsey answered slowly in French so I might follow her: "Marius, I am so sorry. But did you think that I would have mistranslated my husband this afternoon if I had not been sure he would catch me? You see, his ability to understand and speak French and other languages is in fact weak, but it improves miraculously when he hears political opinions that rile him."

Another kind of translation served me well: her ability to render WASP into Brooklyn English. On a couple of occasions when I served as department chairman at the University of Rochester, the secretaries caught one of my less than honorable colleagues—then and still a hero of the radical Left—in my office, reading my private papers. Furious, I thought seriously about bringing him up on charges of grossly unethical behavior. And I took special umbrage at his thinking me a fool who, in those days of student hooliganism and indecency, would keep embarrassing material in my office or at home for that matter. Betsey had little if any respect for him, and he hated her. But she cooled me off: "He's shameless, but you do not want to destroy his career." I acceded to her wishes, as I often did, but poured out my wrath to a respected colleague with solid professional ethics. He went blank, replying, "He exhibited poor form." At that point, I wanted to shoot my valued colleague along with the wretch I was complaining about. I raved to Betsey: "Poor form! Poor form? What is he talking about? What is he made of?" Once again, she cooled me off: "My father, whom you love and admire, would have reacted similarly." Stunned, I asked if she were joking. "Not at all. It's just another of those cultural differences that he and you like to tease each other about. 'Poor form' is the equivalent of your 'swinishness,' 'criminality,' and 'infamia.' Gene, believe me, our colleague was telling you that he, too, was outraged."

Mortifying Dependency

My dependence on Betsey's skills did not end with languages. Robert George, Princeton's distinguished political theorist, wrote a moving obituary for Betsey, which included: "Gene was the head of the family. Betsey managed everything." And so she did. The first time Betsey saw me try to balance a checkbook, she gasped. "Gene, please don't be offended, but maybe I should handle our finances." So she did. Afterwards, I even had trouble recalling what bank we used. For a few years I had a separate bank account to pay for her presents. After awhile it became silly since she had to review my accounts at tax time. I gave it up. How bad was I? I barely passed mathematics in college and probably would have flunked if I had not been a member of the Communist Party. The party considered me an important comrade. For one thing, I was the only openly identified party member who could win election to the student council. The party assigned a math whiz to tutor me. I recall his reaction: "Gene, I consider you a brilliant young Marxist, but when it comes to math, you don't have the brains of a six-year old."

Betsey had been an excellent math student. Under the circumstances, a lifelong incompetent like me should never have challenged her to comment on the widely accepted notion that women could not compete with men at the highest levels of mathematics. She did not get mad. Smiling wryly, she held up her thumb: "Well, men might not reach the heights in math either if they had been raised to believe that this is eight inches."

Betsey had easily followed the intricacies of the "econometric revolution" in the historical profession. In 1974, our friends Robert Fogel and Stanley Engerman published their immensely influential two-volume *Time on the Cross: The Economics of American Negro Slavery,* which brought econometrics to the center of the historical profession. Despite having been trained as economists, they wrote the first volume in clear English. The second volume, designed to array evidence for the statements in volume one, consisted largely of equations, graphs, and technical apparatus. Like other historians, I had difficulty in evaluating their calculations. Gross ignorance in statistical methods, economic theory, and mathematics did not, however, prevent many fellow historians from making fools of themselves by launching attacks, most of them stupid, on a book they were incapable of comprehending. I solved my own problem as I solved my linguistic problems, inability to drive a car, balance a checkbook, and much else: I married a woman more talented than I. Betsey patiently took me through the second volume of *Time on the Cross,* translating, as it were, the technical apparatus and equations into English.

In an age of technological innovation, matters did not end there. I am "computer-challenged"—a polite rendering of "a computer idiot." Betsey taught me to use a computer and rescued me on frequent occasions when I screamed, "Help!" But once again, she exposed herself as impish. She bought herself high-grade computers, which she often exchanged for newer and better ones. I got her hand-me-downs, which was fine with me since I restricted myself to simple operations. It took years before a friend noticed that she had started me off with a much more advanced computer than necessary and raised the level every time she changed her own computer. She reasoned that I would learn faster and work better if I started with a more advanced model—so long as she kept me in ignorance of her nefarious scheme. I am, however, proud to announce that not even Betsey succeeded in persuading me to do e-mail or use a cell phone. Her managerial skills spilled over. We lived in three cities during the thirty-seven years of our marriage: Rochester and Ithaca, New York, and Atlanta, Georgia. In each Betsey lined up the best doctor, dentist, and optometrist in residence. All were busy and had trouble squeezing in one more patient. In Atlanta, our physician, nearing retirement, no longer took new patients, and certainly not strangers. In each city we got the best. How? Betsey always tried to emulate the ways of the Lord—even during her days as a professed nonbeliever. Like Him, she moved in mysterious ways. Besides, as I learned when we first met, there was no easy way to refuse her once she made up her mind.

She managed a lot more. Two of our lesbian friends stayed with us on a visit to Atlanta. They take their Jewish faith seriously, and one is studying to be a rabbi. They were distressed at not knowing of a synagogue in Atlanta that would welcome them. Betsey said she would take care of it. In a trice she returned with the name of an appropriate synagogue and rabbi. I asked where she had gotten the information. A Betsey production: She had called the office of the Catholic archbishop and explained the situation. An aide promptly recommended an appropriate rabbi.

Betsey never bugged me about my shortcomings, faults, and idiosyncrasies. But my refusal to learn to drive a car puzzled her, and, before we married, she questioned me. Unwilling to invoke one of the many available excuses—poor reflexes, night blindness, carelessness—I explained: "I have a neurotic fear of driving." She gingerly asked if I would give it a try and let her get someone to teach me. I told her to wait until we had been married a year to see if she still thought it a good idea. When the time came, she said, "Gene, please don't ever get behind the wheel of a car." Even her mother, who thought I embodied perfection, cringed, "Betsey, for heaven's sake, don't ever let Gene drive a car."

Pleasures and Conversations

We enjoyed doing things together, apart from professional and political matters. In particular, we loved to shop together. Neither of us thought of wearing anything the other disapproved of. It would have made no sense since in large part we dressed to please the other. Each of us thought the other had good taste; understood the other's preferences; and valued each other's opinion. In Betsey's last year or two she could no longer maneuver through Saks, Neiman Marcus, and her other favorites. Several employees who usually attended to her sent clothing to our home for her to keep or send back. They knew her tastes and had some idea of what I would approve or veto. And they alerted her when the best sales periods were on the way. We enjoyed having her model for me at home as we discussed what to keep, but we regretted having to give up the shopping and the accompanying pleasurable lunches out.

Betsey discovered Jo Malone products years ago and had a genius for mixing the scents. I watched as she imaginatively combined them, but initially I thought nothing more than that I much enjoyed the results. I quickly learned that a small army of women—and an occasional man—reacted to her scents. Time after time in shopping centers, restaurants, and other places, women stopped to ask what she was wearing, remarking on how much it enhanced her. I assumed that she had been paying a fortune, for which I had no objection, but she told me that Jo Malone priced her products reasonably. I gather that the world has since discovered Jo Malone, with rising prices a consequence. So long as she maintains the quality, more power to her.

To the fullest extent possible, we did our scholarly reading and writing at home and used our university offices primarily for meeting with students and colleagues. In the last year of her life we gave up our respective studies and turned our living room into a (messy) joint study. Previously, we had separate studies at opposite ends of the house on separate floors so that we might stay close but also have maximum privacy. "Space" was a big word in Betsey's vocabulary. But, increasingly, she had bad falls and waves of weakness. We agreed that I had to stay as close to her as possible. To our pleasant surprise, the diminution in privacy no longer seemed important. We enjoyed the proximity more than we ever imagined. Maybe we enjoyed it in consequence of our getting old. But I am not so sure. I wonder if we would not have enjoyed it many years earlier.

How did we settle on our work routines and mutual responsibilities for housekeeping? I cannot answer properly since we rarely discussed such matters. Until the last year or two of her terrible illnesses we lived in accordance with routines we were hardly conscious of. Both of us were early risers who had a quick breakfast and got to work as soon as possible without getting in the other's way. We each had a good idea of what the other was doing and did not interfere. Sometimes one of us had a problem that required the help of the other. Then, the one asked to help did so without the irritability that interruptions may invite. We pretty well knew what the other faced and tried not to impose. But what if the one who was being asked to help was also jammed up? On rare occasions a matter could not be taken care of, in which case the work of one of us suffered. Again, what was there to discuss? We always knew that the other would stretch to help as much as possible. One mutual practice softened the blow. Each of us could feel when the other was in worse shape, even marginally.

We discussed some things in a kind of shorthand. Through the first twenty-plus years of our marriage, Betsey and I smoked. She smoked Nat Sherman cigarettes in restaurants but cigarette-sized cigars at home and at school. (The ecofascists had not yet succeeded in banning smoking on campus.) I alternated Nat Sherman cigarettes with Schimmelpeninck panatelas. As the years went by, I quit drinking hard liquor but unintentionally increased my smoking until I became a chain smoker. Betsey had to stop smoking after the onset of MS, assuring me that secondary smoke did not bother her. She could not bear the thought of depriving me of my special pleasure, but one evening, as we were watching TV in bed, I noticed that she was uncomfortable. I asked her to tell me frankly if my smoking bothered her. She denied it, but when I looked skeptical, she conceded that, although my cigars did not bother her, my cigarettes seemed to. She wondered if I might restrict myself to cigar smoking in the bedroom, insisting that the rest of the house was not a problem. Uh-huh. I thereupon did what she would have done had our circumstances been reversed. I quit smoking.

We tried to adjust to each other's strengths, weaknesses, and circumstances. When I carried heavy and emotionally draining responsibilities as chairman of the University of Rochester's Department of History, Betsey did everything she could to take pressure off me at home. When her turn came as director of Women's Studies at Emory University, I did everything I could to take pressure off her. I do not recall that we ever discussed relative responsibilities. Neither do I recall a single tense exchange over such matters. Primarily, we each tried to lighten the other's load. Still, in retrospect I fear that for many years I let her take on much more than she should have. For one thing, I had every disingenuous husband's excuse: She was so much more competent than I in just about everything. She thought so, too, and often preferred to do a job herself than have me do it poorly. With me in mind, she liked to paraphrase Frances Butler

Leigh, who ran a plantation in Georgia during post-slavery Reconstruction: "If you want a husband to do something, first tell him what to do, then show him how to do it, and, finally, do it yourself." I think I improved a lot over the years. She said so emphatically, and I pray that she spoke truly.

We had the advantage of being able to spend more time together than most husbands and wives. What did we talk about? History? Politics? Literature? Religion? One subject towered over all: Baseball. We were fanatical fans, poring over the scores and standings every day, and spending much of the off-season following the "Hot Stove League"—the baseball rumor and gossip mill and the record of off-season player trades and other personnel changes. Betsey was a Yankee fan. Despite having been raised in Brooklyn, I have been a Giants fan all my life. We rooted for each other's team easily enough since they are in different leagues. But we worried that both teams might win their respective pennants and face each other in the World Series. Our marriage was built to survive just about anything. But a Yankees-Giants shoot out? Betsey, deferential wife that she was, promised that, if the Giants won, she would be a good sport and celebrate with me. She may have believed what she was saying, but I knew better. Like George Steinbrenner, she refused to believe that the Yankees ever had to lose a game. She expected them to win 162 games a year and sweep through the post season. Anything short of that meant a collapse of the divinely predestined natural order. In baseball matters, as in chess, she was one sore loser.

When I first met Betsey, she rooted for the Boston Red Sox. The poor thing was desolate when the Yankees' Bucky Dent hit a dramatic home run to deprive the Red Sox of the 1978 American League pennant. She became a Yankee fan about a dozen years into our marriage, when we were living in Ithaca. She wrote a marvelous review-essay on baseball wives for the *Village Voice*. Well, what she wrote was marvelous but the resident feminists published a version that reversed her conclusions without consulting her. Doing the necessary research on her subject, she learned that, even by the embarrassing standards of the 1950s and after, the Red Sox had established a reputation for racism. Their players had also established a reputation for cheating on their wives a good deal more than the players on other teams. Indignant, she jumped ship. Well, so she said. I believed her but not without some suspicion. We saw the Yankees on TV when we lived in Ithaca. They had a young, talented shortstop. Andre Robertson looked certain to have a great career if he stayed healthy. (An automobile accident soon wrecked his career.) Pleased as I was to find my wife an acute judge of baseball talent, I noticed that she could not take her eyes off him. I asked her if Robertson was not just handsome, but a veritable Adonis. She grew pensive. Finally, she allowed that she supposed some women might find him attractive.

Our Species-Challenged Persons

Our dogs and cats brought Betsey incalculable pleasure. Betsey loved them and engaged them in conversations of improbable length. I had no problem with her doting on them, but sometimes she threw me. I asked her for the reason she allowed Texas to roam outside at will but kept our other cats indoors. Although I granted that Texas, a tough cat, handled himself on the street, I could not understand her decision. Mystified by my denseness, she enlightened me: "Because he's a boy cat." Without ever coming home with so much as a scratch, he proved himself a natural killer of chipmunks, birds, assorted varmints, and even an occasional squirrel. As cats will do, he proudly brought home his prey as presents. Betsey took it in stride, the more easily since I cleaned up the messes. But even she lost patience when Texas killed a dazzling, bright-red young cardinal. She threatened to roast and feed him to the dogs if he killed anything so beautiful again. That incident aside, Betsey saw no reason to take umbrage at our having a serial killer in our home. "God made him a male cat. Male cats are street warriors. As street warriors go, he is a hero. That's his nature. What am I supposed to rebuke him for?"

Betsey wanted a dog, ostensibly to protect our five—or was it seven?—cats in case of a Martian invasion. I said, "no." Flatly. We were living in Ithaca, which meant long winters and unrelieved snow. I knew who, in the end, would walk the dog. I always loved dogs, whereas Betsey had to overcome my resistance to cats. I learned to appreciate them, but I knew how much more time and effort a dog required. I assumed my proper, authoritarian, patriarchal stance: "And no means no!" One day she went off with a friend to the farmers' market and returned with a puppy. The puppy was not much bigger than our largest cat, but he had huge paws, which signaled that he would be a big dog. He grew to be ninety pounds with teeth as large as I have ever seen on a dog. He turned out to be so handsome that people asked his breed. Well, he was a mutt: half golden receiver, one-quarter Afghan, and one-quarter dober-person. I was furious. She had promised me she would not get a dog without my consent, and then she broke her word. I could not believe it. My Rock-of-Gibraltar wife betrayed me. It was the only time I recall her breaking her word to me over anything of consequence.

Seething, I poured myself a martini, went into the study, and turned on the TV. Then the patter of puppy feet came down the hall. The puppy curled up at my feet, looked up at me plaintively, and settled down to watch a baseball game with me. That is my version. In hers, she put him in a basket and placed him at my feet. One way or the other, I wilted. Betsey apologized profusely for her rashness. I forgave her, and all that. He turned out to be a great dog and a joy to both of us. I came to appreciate him all the more when she took him to school with her. Her drive from Ithaca to Binghamton, where she was then teaching at the State University of New York, took a long hour, and driving in winter through lightly populated areas meant

1990s with Josef

taking risks. With Josef in the car, I no longer had to worry. He was the gentlest of dogs, but I had no doubt that he would rip the throat out of anyone who tried to harm the mistress to whom he quickly had become bonded. Still feeling guilty about her act of treachery, Betsey gave me the privilege of naming the dog. I would teach her a lesson. I named him Josef V. and left her to explain the name to inquirers. A Carlist (monarchist) friend of ours assumed that he was Josef the Fifth and refused to hear that V. stood for Vissarionovich. Josef was a lively, mischievous, affectionate dog—nothing like his namesake— and for eleven years he brought us constant enjoyment.

Betsey loved all the cats and the dogs we had over the years, but her love for Josef had no parallel. I never knew whether she loved him more for his affectionate nature, his companionship, or his mischief. We and Betsey's parents were having a drink before dinner, and I put a generous portion of prosciutto on the cocktail table. Josef lurked, studied the scene, and pounced, swallowing the whole portion in one gulp before we could move. He looked so proud of himself. Despite my best efforts, I could not get mad, and Betsey, although annoyed by his behavior, did not hide her touch of pride.

When Betsey took Josef to school, he did two things that I did not believe when told. Betsey left ten minutes at the end of each lecture for questions and comments. If she went on too long, Josef, to the laughter of the class, stood up and yawned. Similarly, in seminar, Betsey took and gave her students a fifteen-minute smoking break half-way through a three-hour seminar. If she dared delay the break, Josef barked. Did I believe these stories? No, of course not—until I saw them for myself, and her students assured me that the scene re-curred often. Josef's death raised Texas in our eyes. When Josef was dying of cancer, Texas curled up with him, comforting him during his last few days.

My Autobiography

To the annoyance of my wife and others, I have kept few personal papers. I never expected a serious scholar to waste time on my biogra-phy, and I did not want anyone to delve into my private life. In retro-spect, I think I made a mistake. I corresponded with some prominent people from all over the world, and I ought to have thought about their biographers' need for access to correspondence. Several times I had to tell biographers that I no longer had the letters they wanted to see. Improbably, I received several invitations from publishers over the years to write my autobiography. I laughed. With so few records, I could not have written it even if I had thought—as I did and do not—that it would be worth my time or appeal to anyone except as-sorted gossip-mongers and a few old friends.

My adoring wife had other ideas. She persisted in the fantasy that my autobiography would enrich a forever-grateful world. She had the perfect solution: She would write it. My autobiography, mind you, not my biography. Taken aback, I wanted to know how she planned to do it—even fraudulently—without personal papers. I reminded her that she knew little about my life before we met. She twitted me with Aristotle's dictum that art is truer than history. Although she knew few facts about my early life, she intended to construct an accurate account from her imagination. Now, Betsey was hardly a postmodernist. From her father's materialism and from Marxism she retained a commitment to "objective reality." Yet, I suddenly grasped that *Signora Testadura* might actuate her preposterous pronouncement, proceeding on the principle of *se non è vero, è ben' trovato* (It may not be not true, but it's well founded). In truth, Betsey knew me better than anyone ever has come close to knowing me, but I doubt that even she could have imagined, much less reconstructed, my childhood and adolescence.

When I asked Betsey to marry me, we exchanged caveats. Betsey warned me that she had a fatal flaw: "There is something you need to know. I'm crazy." I could not believe my ears. I finally met a sane, emotionally stable woman, and she tells me she's crazy. I accused her of bragging. "I have seen crazy women up close—I mean real close." (Yes, I had.) "You do not begin to qualify. You're nothing more than a garden-variety neurotic like the rest of us." I cured her of that vanity, but at a cost. A year or so into marriage, she began to think, with greater plausibility, that it was she who had married a nut.

I, too, had a caveat. The Italian girls back in Brooklyn were not far off. I have always qualified by reasonable standards as a "drip," although for years I worked with some success to hide it. "I am not gregarious. My life in Manhattan and Montreal was a façade. I prefer minimal social contact and live most of my life in my head." She tried to suppress laughter: "Really! I never would have guessed it. Gene, it's probably the most obvious thing about you. I knew as much from our first evening together or soon after." I replied that I did not think other people saw me that way. "No doubt, but if I were among their number, you would not be asking me to marry you." Betsey had her own interpretation: "Of course you talk to yourself a lot and do not much like to see people. After all, you're the most interesting man you know." I started to defend my honor, but her teasing silenced me or, rather, set me to laughing along with her.

For years James Crawford—our factotum, who runs the house three days a week—and house guests, who stayed with us from time to time, had sport in recounting how I turned the house into a mausoleum whenever Betsey was traveling and how I became a bundle of joy when she returned. In 2004, although Betsey's health was slipping, she helped the pro-life committee of our parish, Immaculate Heart of Mary Catholic Church, as much as she could. In a letter to the excellent woman who chaired the committee, she explained her reasons for not attending evening functions:

> My husband is eleven years older than I and retired. He is in excellent shape and continues to write at an amazing level— and we are writing a good deal together—but he is alone for much of the day. Although he has seemingly endless internal resources and an unimaginable ability to stay at home all day, adventuring inside his own mind, he is deeply committed to my company. I finally figured out that I am rather like the air he breathes—essential as a presence, as I am committed to him. But I am considerably more engaged with the outside world— friends, students, colleagues, even the group at daily morning Mass. Bottom line, I feel I owe him my evenings.

When Betsey met my radical left-wing political associates in New York, she rubbed her eyes. Some of the men and most of the women hated her on sight. Their hostility did not bother her much since she judged most to be overgrown junior-high-school girls. After awhile, she asked, "Am I wrong in thinking that your radical friends in New York do not have the slightest idea of who or what you are?" I told her that they were political associates, not friends. Years of experience had taught me to distrust them and to recognize their professions of friendship and good will as pretense. (Their disgusting treatment of Betsey removed any lingering doubts.) I asked Betsey to remember that I functioned in a political not a social world: "You are dead right, but I have to work with them. So, please do me a favor and keep it to yourself."

3

Nature and Grace

Her will became pliant material for the divine will, and guided by
this will, it could set about taming and curtailing her nature to chan-
nel the inner form. Her will could also find an outer form suitable
to its inner one and a form into which she could grow without losing
her natural direction. And so she rose to that perfected humanity,
the pure consequence of a nature freed and clarified by the power of
grace. On these heights it is safe to follow the impulses of one's heart
because one's own heart is united with the divine heart and beats
with its pulse and rhythm.

—Edith Stein [Saint Teresa Benedicta of the Cross], "The
Spirit of St. Elizabeth [of Hungary] as It Informed her life."

Conversion

Betsey's parents were nonbelievers and reared her accordingly. She
entered the Catholic Church in her early fifties. Previously, she had
never professed a religious faith, although she wished she could have.
Despite her professed materialism, she yearned for spiritual communion in a church that she could enter in good conscience. She had
been unable to bring herself to believe in God, but she never felt
at peace with her unbelief. She disregarded agnosticism as a hope-
less evasion, agreeing with Friedrich Engels' characterization of it as
"shamefaced materialism." Betsey was a decisive woman: There was

nothing shamefaced about her. For most of her life she chose materialism over alternatives, albeit with misgivings.

I, too, had sought spiritual communion, but in a different kind of church—the Communist Party. After my expulsion from the Party in 1950, I remained a Marxist and a supporter of the "movement." Betsey and I had embraced Marxism by different routes. Some small ironies here. Her atheist father imbibed the materialism of the French Enlightenment—what Marxists call "mechanical materialism," in contradistinction to the "dialectical materialism" that Marx extracted from Hegel's dialectical idealism. A man of the New Deal Left, Ed Fox had been appointed by Franklin D. Roosevelt to the State Department, serving briefly as Assistant Secretary of State for policy analysis under Harry Truman. He was a firm Cold War anticommunist liberal. His daughter's embrace of Marxism and sympathy for Marxist political movements made him uneasy. Betsey respected a number of American left-wing radicals but not the great majority. Her sympathies, like those of her parents, lay with working people. Like her husband, she abhorred the cultural radicalism of the New Left of the 1960s, with its open contempt for the working class. During the war in Vietnam, the pampered bourgeois students who were ready to burn down campuses to avoid the draft denounced prowar workers as "sellouts" and "pigs."

Betsey had a larger problem. An acute student of Marx and Marxism, she found the American Left intellectually shoddy and, worse, devoid of moral and ethical criteria. She and I agreed on the intellectual shoddiness and discussed the moral problem many times, always returning to Dostoyevsky's haunting statement: "If God does not exist, then all is lawful." The more Betsey studied, the more convinced she became that the Left had no moral grounding. But without belief in God, she could not respond, in good conscience, to the sense of community our churchgoing friends had. Not that she—and I—were not subject to temptations. Almost from the beginning of our marriage, Episcopalians, Unitarians, and communicants of other churches invited us to join. When we explained that we were atheists, they assured us that belief in God was unnecessary. We paraphrased Groucho Marx: We would not think of entering a church that would have us. Flippancy aside, I knew that Betsey was searching for more than earthly community. We used to joke that we may have been the only American Marxists who believed in original sin and human depravity. It was no joke, but neither was it necessarily accurate. We did believe in the essentials of original sin, as we understood them, but could not square it with our materialism. I am reminded of the outburst of a fellow Marxist and atheist, a superior historian from a Jewish family. We were having a cup of coffee with several Marxist graduate students, who seemed confused by our professed belief in original sin. After a while, they turned to our colleague and asked if he agreed with us. He scowled: "I don't know anything about Christian theology or original sin or anything else they are talking about. But this I do know: People are rotten." I should add that although I may have agreed with him on the rottenness of people—I plead the Fifth—Betsey did not. She was not yet close to conversion, but she had an intuitive grasp of the Resurrection and redemption.

In 1994, at age fifty-three, Betsey announced her conversion. I was not taken by surprise since I always knew she had a marked spiritual side. Contrary to the nonsense spewed across the academic rumor mill, her decision had nothing to do with politics. I asked what church she was planning to enter, assuming that it would be the Presbyterian. In Atlanta we had occasionally attended Peachtree Presbyterian Church to hear excellent preaching, which eschewed feel-good pap for "Christ and Him crucified." Then too, Betsey's father's family had Calvinist roots. Betsey answered, intending no disrespect for the Presbyterian Church or any other: "You have lived with me for about a quarter of a century, and you take me for an evangelical Protestant?" She explained that she was inquiring about instruction to enter the Catholic

Church. I was relieved. Although not prepared to reenter the Church, I had started to think about it and did return in 1995. Betsey later confessed—only a bit tongue-in-cheek—that she had another reason for her choice: "I knew that sooner or later you would return to the Catholic Church and thought we should worship together."

Betsey had long prepared herself to enter the Catholic Church, albeit not consciously. Her nonbelieving parents had sent her and her siblings to Sabbath school wherever they lived. Historians themselves, they understood that, although their children did not have to become historians, they did have to know history. Ed and Betty Fox did not have to be told that Western civilization could not be understood as other than a Christian civilization, and that Christianity could not be understood apart from its roots in Judaism. An understanding and appreciation of Western literature depends heavily on knowledge of its countless biblical allusions. The Foxes sent their children to a Protestant Sabbath school of any denomination, so long as it offered the best Bible study available. They also sent their children to schools in France and Switzerland. Betsey attended a renowned Huguenot school in a small town in the Midi, the inhabitants of which had saved the lives of thousands of Jews from the Nazis at the risk of their own. For the rest, she had studied in-depth medieval history, a subject she loved.

Beneath these practical experiences lay a spiritual journey, the outcome of which appeared in a notebook she kept on an Opus Dei retreat at Murray Hill Seminary in Boston, May 24, 2002. She asked herself what image she had of God. Conjuring up the Old Testament projection of a tyrant, she wrote, "Those who have that image have not learned the lesson of N.T. [New Testament]: God is our father. Only in Jesus Christ do we come to know ourselves." She quoted St. Anselm: "Lord, teach my heart where & how to seek you."

In 1994, Betsey called Mary Alice O'Connor in New Haven to inquire about getting the right instructor in Atlanta. Mary Alice,

With Father (now Monsignor) Richard Lopez. Betsey received five sacraments on December 9, 1995 (Baptism, Reconciliation, Holy Communion, Confirmation, and Marriage)

mother of Betsey's beloved graduate student Sheila O'Connor-Ambrose, recommended Father Richard Lopez. It was a match made in heaven. Betsey told the story of her conversion in two essays, "Caught in the Web of Grace" (published in *Crisis*), and "Conversion Story" (published in *First Things*). Monsignor Lopez told the story of their meeting in his magnificent sermon at Betsey's funeral, which will appear as an appendix in a forthcoming collection of her religious writings.

When Betsey entered the Church, she had no illusion that her quest for salvation would be easy. To the contrary, she understood faith as hard work. She much admired St. Thomas Aquinas, but identified not with his "I know so that I can believe," but with St. Augustine's "I believe so that I can know." A year or two after she entered the Church, she wrote in her notebook:

> I cannot put what I believe into words other than 'I believe in God the Father . . . his only son, our Lord . . . the Holy Spirit, the Holy Catholic Church, the communion of saints, the forgiveness of sins. . . . ' And those I do believe in, but putting substance on them is gradual. The Gospel helps, Mass helps, prayer

helps. That I can even write this tells me I trust my belief. But I know also that I want it stronger.

In matters of faith, as in much else, Betsey had a treasure trove of sympathy, empathy, and a touch of Dorothy Day's "tough love." Sensitivity she had in abundance, sentimentality none. She never was as hard on anyone as on herself.

Not until Betsey entered the Church and I returned to it did we compare notes on our respective spiritual journeys. We usually had lunch together at home, at which time we read the newspapers, with a few exchanges on the stories of the day. Domestic trouble: She wanted to read the newspapers quietly at lunch; I preferred to chat. She wanted to chat at dinner; I adhered to the silence my father imposed at the dinner table when I was a boy. We compromised. I tried—with minimal success—to keep quiet at lunch; she did most of the talking at dinner. But when we went out to lunch every week or two, we usually discussed our scholarly work. Our principal subjects were southern religious history and Christian theology. In particular, we extensively discussed the Calvinist doctrine of predestination and Federal Theory of original sin, which intrigued us. Looking back, we agreed that something strange had occurred. For the six months or so before Betsey's conversion and my reconsideration of professed atheism, we never talked about religion or theology. Our mutual silence stood in contrast to our usual sharing of thoughts and experiences. Apparently, we had found it difficult to talk about our spiritual tension even to each other until we could settle our thoughts and feelings.

Strange Steps on the Road to Rome

Betsey and I had a few jolts before our spiritual journeys led us to Rome. In the early 1970s, the Catholic chaplains at the University of

Rochester invited us to a public exchange of views with two Catholic colleagues of the radical Left. Liberation theology and other irrationalities were in vogue. It seemed as if some people expected us to light Marxist candles to the blessedness of radical Catholicism. What followed cried out for a Jonathan Swift. We said that, as Marxists and supporters of the international Left, we welcomed a political alliance with radical Catholics but considered an ideological blending of materialist Marxism and Christianity an absurdity. I shall pass over the gruesome details of the exchange. In the end, we were driven to defend Catholic theology against "dissident Catholics" who had no time for the fundamentals of Catholic theology, Church doctrine, and the teachings of the Vatican. So there we were, nonbelievers and committed Marxists, fervently defending the doctrines of original sin and human depravity against professed Catholics who replaced the ostensibly dated teachings of St. Paul, St. Augustine, and St. Thomas Aquinas with those of Jean-Jacques Rousseau and the Karl Marx of the utopian *Economic and Philosophic Manuscripts*—the jejune "early Marx" whom neither Betsey nor I ever took seriously. Having begun on that high note, the "exchange" tumbled downhill. I fumed at the arrant nonsense we were being subjected to. I am a fairly able debater who can get rough and has been known to overdo it. Betsey rarely fumed or got rough. Patiently, she took up our colleagues' apostate twaddle, answering point by point from both Catholic and Marxist doctrine to demonstrate their incompatibility. Although one of them had received training in theology at the University of Notre Dame, Betsey rent him on the teachings of his own Church. As for their flirtation with Marxism, I subsequently had to rebuke her for shooting ducks on a pond. Betsey had a great advantage. Whereas they quickly revealed that they did not know what they were talking about, she read carefully as well as broadly, forgetting little of what she read. She did not have a "photographic memory" or "total recall," but she did have an extraordinary capacity to absorb and sort out information.

Whether the subject was St. Augustine and St. Thomas Aquinas, or Rousseau and Marx, opponents had a hard time matching her command of chapter and verse.

Betsey by no means scorned all Catholic radicals who espoused liberation theology. She came away from an international conference with respect for many of the Latin American adherents. Despite deep disagreements, she valued their intellectual and moral gravitas. But she had little tolerance for the fuzzy-minded outbursts of their American imitators.

The Christian sensibility that Betsey exhibited well before her conversion had its wry side. In 1975, the national Unitarian Church honored me with an award for my book *Roll, Jordan Roll: The World the Slaves Made*. Shortly thereafter the Unitarians in Rochester, where we lived, invited me to speak at their Sunday service on the religion of the slaves. I agreed, expecting Betsey to accompany me, as she usually did. She found some flaccid excuse not to. Now, Betsey knew a good deal about the current Unitarian Church, whereas my knowledge was restricted to its early nineteenth-century history. Having been brought up on Catholic Masses, nothing prepared me for what followed: a large room that resembled a high-school gymnasium; a pleasant woman pastor who opened the proceedings with dignity but without mention of God; a series of announcements from the floor on the scheduled picketing of local businesses for racism or something and requests for signatures on petitions against injustice, oppression, and persons' unpersonhood to persons. I thought I was at a political meeting, and I was. In my talk, I spoke respectfully of religion but identified myself as an atheist who found the evidence of black spirituality in slavery a surprise. The congregation received my presentation warmly, for which I was grateful. But afterwards at a coffee circle, kind people invited me to join their church. I reminded them that I was an atheist. They assured me that their church welcomed atheists and that most of the congregants did not believe in God. Apparently with the intention of putting me at ease, someone asked how anyone could believe in God in view of the constant horrors across the world. Would He have permitted the recent terrible earthquake in Nicaragua, in the aftermath of which the great Roberto Clemente lost his life in an attempt to bring relief to its victims? "Would a good God permit such evil?"

I gasped. How could well-educated and intelligent people talk such rubbish? Stunned and momentarily forgetting my atheism, I responded with an impassioned defense of Christian theology. I may not have believed in God, but I considered their objections an insult to my intelligence. I interpreted their remarks as meaning that God, to be worthy of worship, had to do whatever they wanted Him to—that God had to follow the dictates of their various consciences. I reminded my Unitarian hosts of the words of Genesis 23:50: "The thing proceedeth from the Lord. We cannot speak unto you bad and good." I returned home shell-shocked. A "church" of unbelievers! How could my wife have sent me off unprepared, uninformed, and unprotected? Had I married a sadist? Betsey greeted me with a grin—not a smile, a grin. Her right hand was behind her back. Before I could say a word, she thrust it forward, handing me a stiff double martini: "I think you need this."

Let us be thankful that there are Unitarians and Unitarians. I could cite the pious Jeannette Hopkins, our editor and friend. Then there are churches like the First Unitarian Church in Memphis, Tennessee, which, in the wake of Betsey's conversion to Catholicism, invited her in 1995 to present her views on women in contemporary society. The pastor and congregation received her warmly, and, like Jeannette, much impressed Betsey with their piety and intellectual seriousness.

The Crossing

One Sunday I awoke to find Betsey absent. She had left a message to say that she was off to Mass. When she returned, she found a perturbed husband who asked why she had not awakened him to accompany her. Wide-eyed, she answered that she had no idea I would want to accompany her to Mass and did not wish to impose. She knew very well that no (aspirant) southern gentleman, atheist or no, would fail to escort his lady to church. The next week I attended a Catholic Mass for the first time in about fifty years—except for an occasional wedding or funeral. The changes since Vatican II brought me up short, but, to my surprise, it were as if I had never left. For months we attended Mass together: she as a participant, I as a visitor. I did not cross myself with holy water, genuflect, kneel, or take Holy Communion. But I listened carefully and critically to the homilies. An amused Betsey said that her atheist husband probably paid closer attention to the homilies, outraged at doctrinal lapses, than the many devout Catholics at Mass. Fortunately, we heard doctrinally sound preaching at the Cathedral of Christ the King and at Immaculate Heart of Mary Church, except from occasional visiting Jesuits, who were one more charming than the next—polished, magnetic, and doctrinally appalling.

In particular, we were much pleased with the young priests, recently out of seminaries and testing their wings. At first I blanched. I thought their informal pulpit style worthy of hippies. Betsey saw more clearly. Their informality went hand in hand with doctrinal soundness and the fervor appropriate to it. They touched the young people at Mass without lapsing into bad doctrine. And I had to concede that they did not descend into bad taste.

When Betsey entered the Church, she asked me to have our marriage sanctified—in effect, to have a second wedding. I had not yet returned to the Church but had no objection. When she introduced

74

*December 9,
1995—At a
small reception
at our home
after the
wedding*

me to Father Lopez, I jubilantly told him that I considered a church wedding a great gift since, finally, Betsey would have to promise to obey me. Father Lopez has a good sense of humor, but I do not recall his ever laughing as heartily as he did then. No, the Church exacted no such promises. He recommended that I not try to foist it on Betsey—of all people. I regretted to hear that Pope John Paul II and the Magisterium had sold out to the feminists. In a Christian spirit, Betsey and I compromised. She privately promised absolute obedience to the husband she acknowledged as her lord and master. I thereupon ordered her to do as she pleased no matter what I might insist she do. True to her honorable nature, she never violated her oath. In retrospect, I think she swindled me.

Our wedding Mass turned out to be memorable. It was at that Mass that I finally made my decision to return to the Church. Father Lopez preached a superb sermon. Betsey received four other sacraments that day, three at Mass: baptism, confirmation, confession, and Communion. At confirmation Betsey took the name Teresa, after the great Santa Teresa de Ávila. Her choice of a name was over-determined since she also much admired two other saints named Theresa. After Betsey entered the Church—but before I returned—she and

Sheila exchanged endless praise of Sainte Thérèse de Lisieux, who died of tuberculosis in 1897 at age twenty-four. The ladies, holding their favorite atheist captive, went on about her while we were dining at Nino's. I had never heard of Sainte Thérèse and had no wish to enlighten my ignorance. They had no intention of leaving me in peace to enjoy my *vitello saltimbocca* and *valpolicella ripasso*. To my growing irritation, the incorrigible proselytizers kept singing the virtues of Sainte Thérèse. I momentarily shut them up by announcing the imminent publication my ten-volume masterpiece, *The Sins of Sainte Thérèse*. But I could not shut them up about Edith Stein (Saint Teresa Benedicta of the Cross). Born a Jew in Breslau, Poland, in 1891, she died in a Nazi concentration camp. An accomplished philosopher, she studied with the great phenomenologist Edmund Husserl, who held her in high esteem. She entered the Church in Cologne in 1922 and became a Carmelite nun in 1934. Pope John Paul II canonized her in Cologne in 1997. As Betsey appreciated, when Edith Stein read Teresa de Ávila's autobiography, she said, "This is truth." Betsey read Edith Stein's works avidly, her fascination doubtless reinforced by their common Jewish roots.

A Jew without Bagels and Lox

The "Whiting" in Edward Whiting Fox was a Puritan pastor in seventeenth-century Massachusetts. Betsey told me that the "Fox" came from the illegitimate line of Charles James Fox, the Whig British prime minister. I queried her father, who proudly assured me that the story was true. I snorted, "You WASPs are strange people. If someone accused a Sicilian of descending from a bastard, he would get himself killed." He allowed that, yes, certain differences in ethnic sensibility did separate us. His family in America fought on both sides of what Yankees called the Civil War. I was ecstatic to learn that my wife claimed kinship with Daniel Boone, the Cherrys, the Breckenridges, and other prominent southern families. Betsey qualified for the Daughters of the American Revolution and the United Daughters of the Confederacy, and I urged her to join both. She never found time. I pleaded with her to make time: "Don't you understand that having a wife in the DAR and UDC is the dream of every poor Sicilian boy from Brooklyn?" I must assume that she understood since she usually understood everything at hand. But she offered no word of sympathy and did not want to hear any more about it.

By Jewish law, Betsey's mother and she herself qualified as Jews. Her mother, Betty, was a Simon, a branch of New York's Morgenthau family, one of the most prominent of German-Jewish families in America. Betsey's Jewish grandmother had converted to Christian Science and raised Betty accordingly, but Betty became an agnostic early in life and remained one till her death at ninety-four. The nonbelieving Foxes had given Betsey a Christian education but not a Jewish one, apart from Old Testament study. Betsey was a young adult before she recognized Judaism as a religion. Although not Christians, her parents celebrated Christmas but not the Jewish holidays. At one point, some Jewish friends introduced Betsey to bagels and lox. Indignant, she confronted her mother: "Why have we never had bagels and lox?" Mamma faced Betsey down: "Bagels and lox? My dear, we eat blini and nova." (I loved my mother-in-law but must concede that on rare occasions she succumbed to marginal class snobbishness.) Betsey, like her mother, grew up hardly knowing what a Jew was. The holocaust changed everything for them, as for countless other secular Jews. Slowly, without embracing the religion, they identified closely with the Jewish people. Nothing changed for Betsey when she entered the Catholic Church. Year by year she became more conscious and proud of her Jewish origins.

Betsey never did anything to embarrass a host. She never thought of speaking discourteously to, much less quarreling with, a guest in someone else's home. Now, just about everyone took Betsey for a

WASP. Hence, on a couple of occasions at small dinner parties some ass denigrated Jews. Dispensing with her customary good manners and lady-like demeanor, she verbally decapitated him. Embarrassing? Not for her husband, who made no attempt to hide his pride and pleasure. After one of those decapitations I privately accused her of defying the laws of mathematics: "You are 50 percent WASP, 50 percent German-Jewish, and 100 percent Sicilian." She took my remark as the high compliment I had intended. I exaggerated. Since no one incapable of staking out a vendetta qualifies as a true Sicilian, Betsey did not fully qualify.

Working in the Church

When Betsey committed herself to anything, she did so wholeheartedly. When she committed herself to the Church, she dedicated herself to serving it. She became a Eucharistic Minister, assisting the priest at Mass in the administering of Communion. I remember how strange it seemed the first time I received the Host at my wife's hands. And she became a lector. At Mass, laymen read two biblical selections before the priest reads the text for his homily. The lector's instructions call for reading carefully without oratorical theatrics or any attempt to call attention to oneself. A lector presents the Word of God unadorned. By common consent, Betsey read beautifully. At every Mass, parishioners stopped to tell her how pleased and edified they were by her readings. On Sunday afternoon, she spent an hour or more at Perpetual Adoration of the Blessed Sacrament, discontinuing her service only when it became physically impossible.

She had for years lectured widely for Catholic and Protestant groups and written for Christian publications on a variety of subjects, most often on abortion. Perhaps none of Betsey's writings drew as much comment or earned as much admiration as her writings on religion and related subjects. Well before she converted to Christianity and entered the Catholic Church—while, that is, she adhered to materialist philosophy and spoke as a nonbeliever—she attracted attention across the country for her incisive criticism of abortion and defense of the "culture of life." Her reputation spread among Protestants more than among Catholics, at least until she entered the Church. From that point on, her Catholic audience swelled but so did her Protestant.

Abortion had always made Betsey queasy. For years she remained sufficiently attached to the feminist movement to persuade herself to support "free choice" during the first trimester and with such limitations as parental consent and absolute denial of partial-birth abortion. She supported such "compromise" largely because she considered it the best politically available alternative to an incipient civil war. She gagged on abortion for a simple reason: She knew, as everyone knows, that an abortion kills a baby. Betsey responded with incredulity to the argument that the baby a woman carries in her womb is not a baby at all or, alternatively, that although it is a baby, her mother has a moral and constitutional right to kill her. And Betsey resented the denigration of women implicit in the "pro-choice" campaign. Years later, in the private journal she kept after she entered the Church, she wrote:

> Paradox: intent of abortion has been to free women, but it has imprisoned them. *Anima Christi:* soul and body are one, not two. Abortion devalues and debases woman's bodies—strips them of their character as Temples of the Holy Spirit. Abortion has not heightened respect for woman's bodies, but only confirmed their status as objects to be used.

A related matter went down hard with her. We hear all the time that retarded and deformed children should never have been born— that their lives should have been snuffed out by parents and doctors sensitive to the "quality of life." Betsey did not take well to people who claimed the privilege of judging who deserved to live and who ought to be put to death. Again, as a Jew aware of the underlying ideology of the Holocaust, she had no tolerance for people who claimed the right to dispose of human life in accordance with whatever sick creed they were espousing. Over the years, she met a number of retarded and autistic children. None struck her as floating miserably in a life without pleasure. Betsey saw for herself that, however painful their daily experiences, they awoke every morning secure in the knowledge that their parents loved them, considering them gifts of God.

The radical feminists' assertion that a woman has absolute property in her own body provoked mirth from those who, like Betsey, knew that the modern Left had arisen to oppose the bourgeois theory of absolute property in anything. Betsey steadily hardened her line against abortion while she maintained unsparing compassion for the unmarried young or poor pregnant women who felt trapped. She spent years as a volunteer in community groups that cared for pregnant teenagers, poor mothers and their children, and battered wives.

On these matters, as in others, she had special powers of persuasion. I caught a glimpse of her ability to touch an audience in January 2005—less than two years before she died. I attended her lecture on abortion at Hamilton College in New York. She had been invited by the small conservative student contingent, but she faced a large and largely skeptical audience. Once again, I thought she might have spoken in livelier fashion; once again, she refused to indulge in rhetorical tricks or cheap shots, much less talk down to students. She took up the major arguments, pro and con. Calmly, she reviewed moral, statistical, and other evidence and dug into the implications and ramifications of the slaughter of millions of infants. I watched the students closely. Apparently, most did not support her pro-life position, yet they hung on her every word. She may not have convinced many, but she clearly made them thoughtful. And they responded respectfully. It was obvious that their radical feminist professors had not deigned to introduce them to the pro-life side, so that they might "choose" between the alternatives. As the students left the hall, they did not disguise their admiration for Betsey's presentation and replies to hard questions. They also made clear that they were not amused at their professors' efforts to shut them out from an opportunity to consider pro-life views.

Betsey's soft and indirect methods of persuading people to reconsider their positions illustrated her superior skills, and I am afraid that I did not help much. Professor Pamela Hall, speaking at Emory's memorial meeting for her, captured the difference. Describing our dinners at Nino's, she reported, "They both waged an affectionate battle to persuade me to rejoin the Catholic Church. Gene said once: 'Perhaps the Holy Spirit put me here to ask you these questions.' I must have looked desperate for a suitable response. Betsey intervened, 'Well, that would be a most unexpected manifestation of the Spirit.'"

Betsey expected to work with Opus Dei. Declining health prevented her from doing much, but she treasured Opus Dei retreats. I was not happy about her making tiring trips to Boston, and I hated her being away for the better part of a week once or twice a year. I knew that I had no right to object to her retreats and that she would not have rolled over if I had tried. But I knew something else: Although the retreats were tiring, physically and emotionally, she always returned happy and re-energized. When, after her death, I found her private notebooks, I had a better idea of just how spiritually and intellectually refreshing the retreats were. Her notebooks proved revealing. Betsey usually spent more than an hour at confession. Feigning outrage, I demanded to know what terrible sins she had been committing. I hardly suspected her of terrible sins but I did wonder about the time she took. When I read her notebooks, I grasped, as

I had not quite grasped before, the extent and depth of her spiritual quest for her salvation—and mine.

Attendance at retreat constituted a small part of a larger inconvenience. For many years Betsey spent a good deal of time on the road, although whenever possible, she returned quickly, on the same day or the next. She was deluged with speaking invitations from campuses and churches, as well as trade unions, women's groups, business organizations, and community groups. She accepted minimal honoraria or none at all from churches, trade unions, and worthy community groups that she knew to be strapped for money. She often attended professional conventions. The leading professional organizations in modern languages, American studies, English studies, psychology, religious studies, sociology, and political science invited her to participate in their programs. When I first met her, she was a bit queasy about flying. By the time she turned fifty or so, she was a Delta Airlines "Million Mile Flyer."

Accepting the flexibility of the Church's anti-Fundamentalist "development of doctrine," Betsey trusted the pope and the Magisterium to guide us through biblical obscurities and ambiguities. She hued to theological and doctrinal orthodoxy, as Catholics understand it. Her shifting position on women priests made that clear. Long before Betsey entered the Church, Catholics—I do not recall exactly who—invited her to comment on the question of women priests in a forum. She was reluctant to do so since neither she nor I believed in telling Catholics how to be Catholic, any more than we welcomed interventions from non-Marxists who wanted to instruct us on how to be good Marxists. What impertinent white person would any longer have the audacity to try to tell blacks how to be black or how they should run their organizations? With qualms, she accepted the invitation. She presented an analysis designed to demonstrate that the Church, according to its own principles, could admit women to the priesthood. I doubt that she convinced her hosts, but I know that she shook them. When she entered the Church, she did a one-hundred-eighty-degree turn, rejecting her own interpretation and becoming unalterably opposed to women priests. When I challenged her on the strength of her own previous argument, she replied that, as a non-Catholic, she had not taken proper account of the theological grounding of the Church's position. She stood firm on the scriptural grounds for a male priesthood. I conceded the force of her argument but cannot help thinking that Betsey would have made a great pope.

When the time came for Betsey to enter the Church, she had no problem with its structure, which she had studied thoroughly long before her conversion. "Liberal" and "progressive" religion held no attractions. She much admired Pope John Paul II, as did millions of Catholics and non-Catholics throughout the world, and she wrote a good deal in support of his wise pronouncements on women and the Church. She also much admired Joseph Cardinal Ratzinger (Pope Benedict XVI). Had she and I voted in the College of Cardinals, Cardinal Ratzinger would unquestionably have been our first choice. She hoped her prayers for his election would be answered; I doubted that a man of his doctrinal firmness and frankness could make it. When the news came, I rushed to tell her, and we opened a special bottle of wine at dinner to toast His Holiness. I much regret that she did not live long enough to write about the new pope and his doctrinal pronouncements. Years before Betsey entered the Church, she recognized him as an exceptional theologian—the finest in recent memory to grace the papacy.

Betsey read and wrote for her favorite religious journals. And she kept up with books on the current church. She favored the "traditionalist" wing of the Church, although not as dogmatically as I. In particular, she refused to support my proposal to restore the Inquisition and the *auto-da-fé*. Betsey entered the Church in the same spirit as I returned to it, prepared to submit to the authority of its hierarchy. The Catholic Church is an elective monarchy, not a republic, much less a democracy. An honest Christian who cannot accept submission to the hierarchy is at liberty to join the Baptist Church or some other worthy Christian church. He is not at liberty to try to wreck our Church by pretending that it is or should be a "participatory democracy." In any case, Betsey's faith grew stronger year by year, and I have no doubt that she prayed as Jesus taught us: "Thy will be done."

4

Academia and the Public Square

When you find a man who is a Christian praising God by the excellence of his work do not distract him . . . Let him serve God in the way to which God has called him. . . . He is there to serve God by serving his work.

—Dorothy L. Sayers, *Creed or Chaos*

After the announcement of Betsey's death, I was deluged with hundreds of written and oral communications from coast to coast and from people in every walk of life. I appreciated the condolence cards but was taken off guard by the great majority of the cards, letters, and conversations—eloquent tributes that detailed her impact on individual lives. At the reception after her funeral Mass, at Emory's memorial meeting, in numerous telephone calls, and more than two hundred and fifty written messages, people conveyed what they felt they owed her: colleagues and students, public personalities and working people, men and women, blacks and whites, gays and straights, young and old. One feature of the messages brought me up short. I was not surprised that a good many Southerners, conservatives, and old-fashioned chaps referred to her as a "Great Lady." To my great surprise, that very expression came from a number of people on the Left, indeed the radical Left. I could not recall ever having heard it in those circles.

2003: A Glorious Year

To Betsey's amazement, in the Year of Our Lord 2003 President George W. Bush appointed her to the Governing Council of the National Endowment for the Humanities. Also in 2003, she received a National Humanities Medal from the White House, as well as a special commendation from Georgia's State Senate, the Cardinal Wright Award from the Fellowship of Catholic Scholars, and (jointly with her husband) the Intercollegiate Studies Institute's Gerhart Niemeyer Award for Distinguished Contributions to Scholarship in the Liberal Arts. When the White House announced her medal, I was ecstatic, she incredulous. Not in a million years did she expect such an honor. She could not imagine what she had done to deserve it or the other awards that came in a rush.

The citation, signed by President Bush on November 14, 2003 provided a succinct answer:

> The President of the United States of America Awards this National Humanities Medal to Elizabeth Fox-Genovese:
>
> For illuminating women's history and bravely exploring the culture of America's past and present. A defender of reason and a servant of faith, she has uncovered hidden truths and spoken with courage in every chapter of her life.

At the White House, President and Ms. Bush, with Dr. Lynne Cheney, presided over a tasteful ceremony and, although not Italian, provided an exceptionally good luncheon buffet. Dr. James W. Wagner, the new president of Emory, hosted a luncheon to mark the occasion of her medal. A number of her colleagues spoke well. Betsey was moved, as was I. Professor Pamela Hall, Director of Women's Studies, a feminist well to the left of Betsey, described the breadth, solidity, and reputation of Emory's Women's Studies program, commenting, "None of this would have been possible without the leadership of Elizabeth Fox-Genovese. . . . Her intellectual rigor, the elegance of her thought, and her passion for learning set an example for us all."

Subsequently, the Georgia State Senate—no doubt unintentionally—embarrassed Betsey's feminist and radical-left assailants, who charged her with being an ultra right-wing something or other. The Senate unanimously passed a resolution of congratulations, which specified her many contributions to her adopted state. It was introduced by Senator David Adelman, a prominent liberal Democratic Party leader.

Georgia State Senate

A Resolution

Commending Elizabeth Fox-Genovese; and for other purposes.

WHEREAS, Elizabeth Fox-Genovese is one of only two Georgians serving on the Governing Council of the National Endowment; and

WHEREAS, since 1990, she has given over 150 invited lectures to university audiences around the country; and

WHEREAS, she has served as general editor of curricular materials for the Organization of American Historians on American women's history; and

WHEREAS, Elizabeth Fox-Genovese has served on a variety of public advisory boards that reflect her interdisciplinary interests, including the Center for Human Life and Bioethics, the Center for Religion and Democracy, and the Society in American Ideals and Institutions at Princeton; and

WHEREAS, Elizabeth Fox-Genovese has shown steadfast dedication to teaching and mentoring of university students, both undergraduate and graduate; and

WHEREAS, she has enhanced the understanding and appreciation of the humanities for countless Georgians; and

WHEREAS, in receiving the National Humanities Medal, Elizabeth Fox-Genovese has brought honor to her adopted State of Georgia and joined a select number of distinguished individuals who have set the highest standards for American cultural achievement; and

WHEREAS, Elizabeth Fox-Genovese has performed an incalculable public service through her extraordinary powers of creativity and vision in preserving, interpreting, and expanding this nation's cultural heritage; and

WHEREAS, the reach of Elizabeth Fox-Genovese's service to scholarship is deep and wide.

NOW, THEREFORE, BE IT RESOLVED BY THE SENATE that the members of this body commend Elizabeth Fox-Genovese for unparalleled scholarship, teaching, service, and cultural contributions to the humanities, the STATE of GEORGIA, and the nation.

BE IT FURTHER RESOLVED the SECRETARY of the SENATE to transmit an appropriate copy of this resolution to Elizabeth Fox-Genovese.

SENATE RESOLUTION 959

By: Senator [David] Adelman of the 42nd.

ADOPTED in the SENATE, March 19, 2004.

Betsey appreciated academic honors, the more so since she never expected them. But I doubt that any gesture meant more to her than Eudora Welty's gracious reception at Millsaps College, a jewel in Mississippi's academic crown. In the 1990s, Millsaps College honored

Betsey twice: once with an honorary degree, and once with an invitation to serve as Eudora Welty visiting professor. To a packed auditorium, she delivered the Eudora Welty Lecture, speaking on the religious life of nineteenth-century southern women. It was a wonderful occasion in several ways. We spent some time with Ms. Welty before the lecture, and she made a lasting impression on us. A great southern lady, she was unpretentious, wry, witty, and gentle but firm in her opinions. I had the honor of sitting with Ms. Welty at the lecture. She made no effort to hide her admiration, indeed enthusiasm, for Betsey's lecture. She turned to me at the end, remarking on Betsey's wonderful grasp and sympathy of her subject. Then Ms. Welty added, almost whimsically, "I am sure that just about everyone assumes she is a Christian. When we move toward the door, pay attention to the comments all around you. You will hear, 'What church do you think she attends?'" And so it happened. Ms. Welty knew that Betsey was a professed nonbeliever, but she was on target: No one could have guessed Betsey's unbelief from her sensitive portrayal of the Christian sensibility of southern women.

An Elite Education

An extraordinary career and the discipline that made it possible began early. Betsey's parents, although by no means wealthy, were well-off. They provided their three children with first-rate educations but refused to spoil them with more money than they needed. Betsey attended North Country School and Concord Academy in the United States and elite schools in France and Switzerland. As a girl, she had no idea of her family's financial condition. The Foxes arranged tuition, kept their children properly dressed, and provided advantages that working-class youth would envy. Yet, their children were always conscious of having much less spending money, cars, and just about everything than the rich young people they went to school with.

Betsey as a senior at Bryn Mawr

From the beginning they learned thrift and prudence and expected that, as adults, they would have to provide for and rely on themselves.

I am grateful for the solid education I got in Brooklyn at PS 201 and New Utrecht High School, but it could not substitute for the elite education that Betsey received at private schools in America and Europe. Still, countless young people go through elite schools with minimal or average profit. They do not benefit fully because they take their privileges for granted and do not recognize their social duty to make the most of those privileges. Betsey had been reared to take every opportunity not merely as a challenge but a duty.

Bryn Mawr College provided her with an excellent higher education at the hands of a superior faculty. Betsey loved Bryn Mawr. Her years there convinced her of the value of single-sex education for those who want it. When, in later years, she defended the right of Virginia Military Institute and the Citadel to exclude women, she particularly reacted against the thinly disguised campaign of Janet Reno's Department of Justice to destroy single-sex education. Betsey supported women's efforts to attend coeducational or women's military academies and was appalled when the women's colleges cynically refused to rally to VMI and the Citadel, thereby scuttling their support for single-sex education. She sadly viewed the intellectual and professional course of most of the prestigious women's colleges as a betrayal of women.

We all take hard blows in life, whatever our class, sex, or race—whether because of precarious health, gross social inequities, or any number of other circumstances. Betsey took her share in stride. She refused to think, feel, or play the victim. Her experience at Harvard had high moments, particularly in her relations with such distinguished scholars as Franklin Ford and David Landes, but it had dismaying moments as well. Before and during the 1960s, women did not exactly qualify as colleagues in the eyes of their male fellow graduate students. One day a chap approached her. He turned out to be decent enough in later years, but he jarred her at the time. He wanted to know how in good conscience she could seek a professorship and thereby deprive some man with a family to take care of. Years later, that recollection still rankled. All I could do was to resort to the bad language that I used often until I reentered the Church. Then she was told that, to win a teaching fellowship in history, students had to take their comprehensive examinations by a certain early date. She did just that—something not expected of women. Having worked herself into the ground at the expense of her health, she passed with flying colors. Elated, she went to see the departmental secretary, whom everyone considered pretty much the department's boss. She replied, "But dear, you know we don't give those positions to girls." In later years she still could not entirely disguise the hurt. Hurt, not anger. Her health buckled, and she went through a few harrowing years. She eschewed bitterness and quietly pursued her goals and tried to help the young academic women who came up behind her. I do not recall Betsey's having let herself become embittered over anything or anyone, however stern her judgments of people from whom she had expected better. Decades before she entered the Church, Betsey lived as a Christian should. She fought as hard as she could against personal and social injustice and oppression, albeit without unbridled anger.

Harvard was *terra incognita* for me. I never suffered from Ivy League ambivalence, not to say lunacy—a horrible disease that affects certain academics for whom heaven-on-earth consists of Harvard and Yale and hell-on-earth everything else. The Ivy League held no fascinations for me, but neither did I entertain hostility toward it. I never set foot on the Harvard campus until Betsey invited me to speak to her undergraduate seminar. But Harvard had long been a factor in the life of Betsey's family. Her father had gone through Harvard on a Whiting scholarship, named after his seventeenth-century ancestor, and he served as an assistant dean from 1941-45. Her mother earned a B. A. and M. A. from Radcliffe and served as an assistant to William L. Langer, a distinguished Harvard historian. Harvard and "The Academic"—as the Foxes called it—were in Betsey's blood. But not everything went well. She was floored during her first year in graduate school when she enthusiastically praised Eric Hobsbawm's *Age of Revolution*. Her fellow students in graduate seminar sneered: Hobsbawm was a Marxist; he therefore had no standing among serious scholars; she ought not to be wasting the class' time on a historian of marginal talent. Betsey could be silenced for the moment but not be intimidated. She took their bias, not to say stupidity, as a prod to read Hobsbawm's other work. Since Hobsbawm was a Marxist, she concluded that she had better study Marx in depth. As was her wont, she began with Volume One of Marx's *Collected Works* and pressed on. In consequence, she acquired a thorough knowledge of Marx's work, including the more difficult that few American Marxists read: *Grundrisse*, *Capital*, and *Theories of Surplus Value*.

When I met her, I judged her writing style wooden. Harrumphing in a properly male-superior manner, I set out to teach her the ABCs of good writing. I was puzzled by the apparent lack of influence from her father, who was a fine stylist. Then came a shock. I read several of her term papers from Bryn Mawr, and, lo and behold, they were well-written. I could not believe that the woman who had written the papers at Bryn Mawr wrote the papers at Harvard. I reminded myself that most graduate schools seem dedicated to the transformation of the English language into gibberish. In place of clear, straightforward prose, budding geniuses in graduate seminars have to impress their professors with the profundity that only bad writing and vacuous "theorizing" can communicate. Betsey and I reviewed her work together, and it did not take her long to clean up the mess. By the time she began to publish, her prose once again reflected the tutelage that her father and her professors at Bryn Mawr had provided.

At first, I thought that Betsey just could not spell. Frank Tannenbaum, my old professor at Columbia University Graduate School—a great man—once burst out in class: "I can't spell! I just can't spell." But I noticed a peculiar pattern to Betsey's spelling errors. She consistently misspelled only certain words. Studying them, I recognized that they had one thing in common: They were all French cognates. She shook her head when I pointed out the pattern. She immediately identified the root of the problem. Her fancy American schools, good as they were, did not teach everything well, specifically English grammar and spelling, whereas her French schools did teach French grammar and spelling. Her spelling problems thereupon disappeared. Well, almost.

Betsey had her sore points and on one or two occasions burst into tears when subjected to unkindness by someone she never expected it from. But positive reaction to honest criticism remained one of her great strengths. She never resented professional criticism from her husband. And vice versa. We were harder on each other's work than we were on that of others. If either of us had felt rancor or resentment, we could never have collaborated successfully. For us it was easy. We strove to improve and were grateful for any help we could get.

Her Doctoral Dissertation

Betsey's career as a scholar and teacher began curiously. As she was finishing her dissertation, she brought me up short. She decided not to write a final chapter on François Quesnay's attempt to make his *Tableau Économique* balance. I shall spare readers the difficult theoretical problems that lay at the heart of the critical scholarship on Physiocracy. Suffice it that Quesnay had designed the first presentation of economic circulation but could not balance input with outflow. A mathematician, he ended his life attempting to square the circle—literally—and his many interpreters among historians and economists found themselves trying to square the circle that his *Tableau* seemed to have created. Scholars advanced various explanations, including some that denied the problem was soluble. Betsey had an original thesis that blended ideological with economic analysis. Most scholars do not enjoy having their own explanations overthrown by newcomers—and "girls" at that—who explore a major problem in a new way. Betsey, worrying about an onslaught of hostility and ridicule, thought she would eliminate the last chapter of her book and rest her contribution on the secondary light she shed on Physiocracy. That would have earned her a reputation as a good scholar but would have submerged her primary achievement.

I was torn. I did not want to drive her to do something she was reluctant to do, much less into a position in which she could get hurt, maybe badly. But neither did I want her to let it slide. As she often said, I had more confidence in her work than she did. I thought—and she subsequently acknowledged—that she would not have forgiven herself if she had backed off. In such cases, we had a standard procedure: One of us would refrain from campaigning for a specific course but would review carefully the alternatives and probable consequences. (Caveat: what you say is not necessarily as important as the way you say it. I know I never effected a tone that tried to bully Betsey, if for no other reason than that she did not tolerate bullying.) I did not have to do much talking. Betsey believed in her thesis and hated the idea of burying it. After a day or two of reflection, she picked up the gauntlet. To our pleasant surprise, reviewers from all over the world—above all, the most prestigious—greeted her book warmly. In particular, she received thoughtful and flattering reviews from Marxists—notably Marguerite Kuczynski and Ronald Meek, substantial scholars whose work she had respectfully criticized. Madame Kuczynski and her husband, Jürgen, an internationally renowned labor historian, invited her to meet them in England and entertained and encouraged her.

A Prolific Writer

The raw number of Betsey's academic achievements cannot begin to capture the content of her career or the responses to it. Among her lesser-known valuable contributions was her translation of *The Autobiography of Pierre DuPont du Nemours* (1984), for which she supplied a sixty-page critical introduction on the nature and development of autobiography. She wrote five books, which spanned eighteenth-century French history, the history of the Old South, and women's studies: *The Origins of Physiocracy: Economic Revolution and Social Order in Eighteenth-Century France* (1976); *Within the Plantation Household: Black and White Women of the Old South* (1988); *Feminism without Illusions: A Critique of Individualism* (1991); and *Feminism Is Not the Story of My Life: How Today's Feminist Elite Has Lost Touch with the Real Concerns of Women* (1996); and *Marriage: The Dream that Refuses to Die* (2008). She and I coauthored *Fruits of Merchant Capital: Slavery and Bourgeois Property in the Rise and Expansion of Capitalism* (1983); *The Mind of the Master Class: History and Faith in the Southern Slaveholders' Worldview* (2005); and *Slavery in White and Black: Class and Race in the Southern Slaveholders' New World Order* (2008). In addition, several of her lectures were published as booklets, notably *Unspeakable Things Unspoken: Ghosts and Memories in the Narratives of African-American Women* (The Elsa Goveia Lecture at the University of the West Indies, Kingston, Jamaica 1993); *"To Be Worthy of God's Favor": Southern Women's Defense and Critique of Slavery* (The Fortenbaugh Lecture, Gettysburg College, 1993); and *Women and the Future of the Family* (The Kuyper Lecture, 2000). She edited, coedited, or wrote introductions to seven works of history and literature. She served as general editor of, and heavy contributor to, the two-volume *Restoring Women to History* (1984–86), sponsored by the Organization of American Historians, which subsequently did not want to recognize her name while it took credit for her work.

Over the years, Betsey served some twenty journals and projects as editor, a member of the editorial board, contributing editor, or editorial adviser, including journals of broad intellectual content, history, religion, women's studies, and American and southern studies. She appeared on television and radio commenting on election night; the Mike Tyson saga that led to his imprisonment; abortion; her move from Marxism to Christianity; on education in general and women's education in particular; and a variety of other matters.

Her hundred and fifty articles and essays spanned an even wider number of subjects. Her essays on southern women writers and black women writers are being collected in a substantial volume, as are her writings on religion and the Church, including Catholic theology and ecclesiastics, the history of the Christian churches, and specific issues like abortion. At this moment, friends have begun work on a projected four-volume *Selected Writings of Elizabeth Fox-Genovese*.

A Teacher

No feature of her academic life gave Betsey more pleasure than teaching. An earnest: Although Harvard's Department of History

1990s—Betsey on Emory campus with Josef

refused her the teaching fellowship she had earned, the Department of Social Relations invited her to teach. When I was courting her in Cambridge, I picked up a copy of Harvard's student newspaper. It contained an editorial announcement: "Elizabeth Fox will be lecturing tomorrow at 9.00 a.m. [or was it 8:00 a. m.?]. This one will be worth getting up for."

Betsey cared avidly about her students. Her graduate students, with a handful of exceptions, were a joy. I never knew a professor who spent more time with graduate students. Still, she missed the undergraduates, especially the freshmen for whom she had taught seminars. Teaching freshmen, especially in seminar, requires special dedication and talent. It is an art for which I had no talent. I tried—unsuccessfully—to teach freshmen seminars once or twice and beat a retreat to classes for juniors and seniors. Notwithstanding her talent and enthusiasm, she had little choice once she went to Emory. She taught regularly for three departments or more, which needed her help in graduate work. Only occasionally did she teach an undergraduate freshman seminar, although she admitted a few advanced undergraduates to her graduate seminars.

All told, Betsey trained some fifty Ph.D.s throughout her career. At Emory, where she did graduate teaching in English, and women's studies, as well as history, she trained thirty-four, with another half dozen or more "in the pipeline"—that is, at work on dissertations—when she died. She had exceptional ability to place students, male and female, in good jobs. She wrote peerless letters of recommendation. She had a knack of writing at length about a student's strengths, without ignoring weaknesses. Her close attention to detail won the praise of a number of recruitment committees.

I came to know Betsey's students at dinners. For some years we frequently had her seminar students to our home for dinner. But as we grew older and especially when Betsey's health began to slide, we took them to Nino's, our longtime favorite neighborhood Italian restaurant. And every other week or so, she invited one or two students to Nino's for discussions of their seminar work, preparation for orals, and dissertations. She established a reputation for being outstanding in the preparation of students for job interviews. I looked on in wonder as I watched her coach her students in an informal and leisurely way at dinner. Her students were bright and able. She worked them hard but with a gentle touch, as one after another testified. I found those leisurely dinners pleasurable, applying my share of their time to bantering and teasing. I am told that I am a great tease. I do not know. I do know that I enjoyed her students and hope that they enjoyed me. Betsey loved her students and drew immense pleasure from those evenings.

Among her graduate students were a number of black women—one more talented than another. I have been told that she trained more black women Ph.D.s than the whole white humanities faculty at Emory put together. She had an unusual number of women students—black and white—who, having taken years off to raise families, returned to graduate work. They had particular problems, which Betsey fully understood. Recalling her own difficulties as a woman in graduate school, she developed a knack for strengthening the self-confidence of her students, black and white. But she also knew that black women faced problems well beyond those faced by white. She worked hard to understand those problems and to offer the kind of support they called for.

She secured her first academic appointment at the University of Rochester as an entering assistant professor. As such she lacked tenure and could be dismissed at the end of her three-year term with no possibility for appeal. Service workers were trying to unionize, and the university took a hard line. The university is private and expensive. Although it attracts a variety of good students, it also serves as a "backup" for affluent students who do not quite make it into Harvard or Yale. The workers, largely black and Hispanic, had never been through a strike before; initially, they reacted timidly, as is often the case with workers who are facing their first such struggle. Fortunately, Local 1199 had a tough and experienced leadership, and the young organizer assigned to the campus, although inexperienced, showed his mettle. The union's prospects did not seem bright. The students tended to be anti-union or unconcerned, and the professors—with a number of honorable exceptions—were openly hostile or looked for beds to hide under. The leaders of Local 1199 made clear that, although the workers had to win their own struggle, they needed some support on the inside. I shall pass over the details of what turned out to be a rough but brief (one-week) war, won by a quickly toughened group of workers. I did my part and had something extra to offer since, during my teens, I spent summers working with strikers for Communist-led unions in New York. Betsey had no such experience.

Our biggest problem: We had to win the support of enough students to double or triple the picket lines and restrain those students who were spoiling for a fight with the workers. Pro-union professors were hemmed in. We had the respect of many students but not necessarily their affection. We were not well-placed to win them to the workers' cause. Betsey was the exception. Droves of them admired her, including some of the toughest fraternity members. One of the fraternity houses, occupied mostly by Irish and Italian students, many from the more economically secure sections of the working class, had a reputation for housing the roughest students on campus. The administration wanted to shut their fraternity house down. Betsey, although only an assistant professor, intervened, represented their cause before the appropriate committees, and won. She did so in part because she saw immediately that much of the hostility was directed against their rough working-class exterior.

The fraternity's leaders enrolled in her courses on Women's History, primarily to meet "chicks." Before long they took the courses seriously, talking about how much they were learning and how much they respected the professor. At one point Betsey scheduled her women's studies seminar to meet in their fraternity house, which had a splendid living room with an imposing fireplace. The women students, horrified, balked, saying that they would not go near the place, that it was full of rowdies. Betsey guaranteed that the young men would greet them properly. As it turned out, the young men were on their best behavior, served coffee and crumpets, and behaved like gentlemen. When the strike came, some of the other fraternities threatened to gang up on the strikers. Since a number of those anti-union fraternity men were jocks, the threat had to be taken seriously. In response to an appeal from Betsey, the students in our favorite fraternity—who had a reputation for not tolerating disrespect—sent word that they would interpret physical force against the strikers as an unfriendly act.

I shall never forget Betsey's speech from the library steps to a large crowd. Her defiance of the rules against unauthorized meetings could have led to her dismissal. Betsey had antagonists within the administration, but she also had to contend with others who wanted my head. Since I had tenure they could not easily strike at me, but they could strike at Betsey and, in effect, force me out along with her. Once again, I saw her knees shaking. She was a remarkably strong woman but there was nothing "tough" about her. It was her strength rather than toughness that made her cast some things beyond the pale. At a faculty meeting, a scientist announced that the workers had to take care of themselves and that the money they needed for their families would better be spent on his laboratory. Any apprehensions Betsey had about her vulnerability evaporated. She was livid. The veins almost popped out of her neck. On the library steps she laid out the workers' grievances, vividly describing the pain that they and their families were suffering from low wages and a severe inflation. She spoke from what she knew. She spent time with the workers, dismayed by what she heard and saw of their circumstances.

She appealed to the students to accept moral responsibility to defend the people who worked for them and whose families badly needed help. No fireworks, no overwrought rhetoric, no hyperbole. She spoke softly and eloquently, touching her audience. In the next few days the picket lines swelled, and inside the campus the pro-strike students won some hard battles, the nature of which I shall pass over. Betsey's efforts did not stop with a speech. She devoted much of her time to working with the strike committee and supporting students on action inside the campus. When the university caved, the workers raised her aloft as their champion. They appreciated the commitment and militancy shown by some faculty members. They affectionately referred to me as "the crazy Sicilian." Betsey was something else: "that great lady."

Betsey related well to the workers at every university at which she taught: Rochester, SUNY-Binghamton, and Emory. When she died, the cleaning workers at Emory made no effort to hide their grief. Yes, she was unusually generous to the workers at Christmas and on special occasions, but no less important, she showed them genuine respect. And they returned her respect. She knew their names, inquired about their families, and was available when they needed help. (Non-academics might be incredulous at how few professors know the names of the people who clean their offices, much less inquire about their children.) Betsey, like her brother and sister, had been brought up by bourgeois parents to judge people by their character. Whatever the faults of the Foxes, old and young, they detested indifference, condescension, and snobbishness toward working people.

Sidelights

Betsey and I had an enviable reputation among commercial and university publishers of various political stripes, who called on us frequently to read manuscripts submitted to them, making clear that they considered us scrupulously fair. We recommended books on their scholarly merits, no matter what we thought of the authors' politics or worldview or whether we liked them personally. Books we recommended included some that attacked our work. I shared Betsey's reputation for fairness and objectivity, but she outdid me in an important particular. I would like to think that I am a good critic, but I was never in her league. She painstakingly crafted detailed and not easily matched criticisms of content and prose style.

In the early 1970s statistics became part of the historian's training, and Betsey spent a summer studying historical statistics at the prestigious Newberry Library in Chicago. She delivered her customary performance and was invited to return the next year to teach statistical methods to professors of woman's studies. Years later she assisted the lawyers who defended Virginia Military Institute and offered a statistical analysis to demonstrate that the young black males would suffer the most by forced sexual integration. I thought she was stretching and so did the lawyers. She did not argue. She laid out the evidence. The judge singled out her analysis in his ruling, taunting the Justice Department lawyers for having proven unable to refute her.

Betsey, while an associate professor at the University of Rochester, acquired formal training in psychoanalysis. She spent a year at Tavistock Institute in London while I was serving as Pitt Professor at

Cambridge University; she then put in two years in New York at Columbia University's Center for Psychoanalytic Study and Research. To no one's surprise she did well, and her professors urged her to give up history and hang out a shingle. I made no effort to influence her decision, although I did not want her to give up history. She declined to switch, having set out to study psychoanalysis as part of her general education, not out of any desire to practice. She once wrote that she had considered psychoanalysis as a career change, but it never seemed to me that she had done so seriously. I learned something about her self-discipline while watching her study for her courses in psychoanalysis while teaching history half-time at Rochester. I recalled our first meeting, at which she impressed me with her thorough command of the works of Marx. She bought the multivolume *Collected Works of Sigmund Freud*, started with Volume One and read the rest in sequence, not skipping much. She repeated the process with other leading theorists. Her standard procedure.

She learned a great deal from her literary and psychoanalytic studies, which strengthened her work as a historian and benefited her studies of southern women. Some of our new-wave feminist "theoreticians" criticized Betsey for not, in effect, psychoanalyzing southern women, especially enslaved black women. Betsey paid her critics no mind, knowing that they did not have a clue to what they were talking about. But when the most prestigious of southern historians, who had glowingly reviewed her book, *Within the Plantation Household: Black and White Women of the Old South,* pandered to the radicals and echoed their blather, she ceased to be amused. There she was—with advanced academic training in psychoanalysis—subjected to instruction by dilettantes. As usual, she kept her temper. As usual, I did not. She patiently explained that her critics' preferred procedures violated professional procedures and invited a plunge into irresponsible and dangerous speculation. Privately, she remarked: "Can you believe this? They want me—a white woman—to psychoanalyze not only black women but black slave women, and not only black slave women but dead black slave women. What is in their heads?" I made an effort to explain the nature of their heads but not in language she would let me commit to print, much less use herself.

Having good German helped Betsey in her psychoanalytic studies and offered her special pleasure since she had a special attachment to the "beautiful" German language. I found that out the hard way. Shortly before we married, I passed on an Italian joke: "You sing in Italian, write poetry in Spanish, make love in French, and in German you talk to your horse." Her sense of humor failed her: She got mad. One evening in Montreal, we had Rudolf Schlesinger, a visiting professor at St. George University, to dinner. Schlesinger, editor of the British journal *Soviet Studies*, had led quite a life. A respected scholar and a Communist, he risked his life in the anti-Nazi underground. He then took refuge in the Soviet Union and barely escaped when Stalin decided to have him shot for something or other. We talked politics but mostly German literature. He was overjoyed to find that Betsey had good German; that she had read, in German, much of the work of Goethe, Heine, and other literary giants; and that she could discuss the texts in-depth and with ease. I had expected to spend the evening in political discussions with the formidable Dr. Schlesinger. Instead, I had to listen to lively exchanges about great German writers, only a few of whom I had read in translation. Worse, Schlesinger and Betsey could not help speaking in that beautiful German language a good deal of the time, stopping from time to time to tell me what they were talking about.

Madame Defarge

Betsey refused to be intimidated by overbearing men and certainly not by men she knew could not carry her notebook. She had few problems with strong men whom she respected as scholars, colleagues, and capable administrative superiors. More than once she reduced some of her male colleagues to barely suppressed fury. Mind you, she was never brash, discourteous, or disrespectful. She just refused to play the "good girl." Academic women all over the country fell victim to childish spite, but Betsey asked for big trouble by indulging in a horrible excess. At academic meetings, I doodled without arousing resentment. She did needlepoint. She was exceptionally good at it, and her results embellish the walls of our home. She thereby conjured up visions of Charles Dickens' Madame Defarge, who, on the eve of the French Revolution, knitted while savoring the thought of mass executions. The twisting of crossed knees and the looks of distress on the faces of what passed for men were wonderful to behold. I did not take it well, but Betsey refused to get angry. She knew men's foibles well and felt sorry for the pathetic twerps. Come to think of it, she probably felt sorrier for their wives.

Women of Betsey's generation had a tough battle to win acceptance in academia. The sad truth is that confident and accomplished women intimidate all too many male professors. I hope things have improved, but when, in the 1970s and 1980s, women were finally given academic opportunities, strong women often reduced male colleagues to a gnashing of teeth. Betsey was only one of a number of accomplished women academics who scared the wits out of many of the "men" who had to deal with them. For Betsey's amusement, I presented the Genovese Theory of Little-Boy Behavior: "A male who cannot respect a woman as a colleague or a professional superior or work comfortably for a competent woman boss is worried about his performance in bed."

An Enemy of the People

Betsey was much beloved by people across the country and in all walks of life. If her admirers could be assessed quantitatively, they would outweigh many times over the number of feminists and others on the radical Left who hated her. The sheer cruelty attendant upon their hatred outdid anything I have seen in academic politics—and I lived through the McCarthy era as a young Communist. Let me add that any number of fine women, including some of Betsey's colleagues and students, continue to cling to radical feminism—albeit fewer and fewer—in hopes of seeing it transformed into a healthy force. With admiration for their efforts to civilize a barbarous movement, I wish them luck.

Betsey and I married in 1969, and for the next thirty-seven years, neither of us had the slightest doubt that we would spend the rest of our lives together. But what did we know? According to the radical feminists, I married Betsey for her money. Well, of course I did. Why else would anyone have married Betsey Fox? I regret to report that Betsey had no money of consequence. Her mother remarked to me shortly after our marriage, "If my family had not lost its money in bad investments, you would be a rich man today." I sighed with relief. Marrying a rich woman had never been on my agenda and would not have gone down well with my family. In later years the story changed. It seems that unnamed Texas billionaires had staked us to an antebellum mansion in Atlanta, staffed with servants. You might have thought that her assailants knew that General Sherman burned Atlanta and that antebellum mansions are hard to find. For the record, we lived in a middle-class home built in the 1980s. As for a staff of servants: I wish.

To my everlasting regret, Betsey and I never knew any Texas (or other) billionaires, much less any who were willing to support us. Too bad. As we used to say in Brooklyn: "Rich or poor, it's nice to have money." We lived on our earnings. Shortly before Betsey died, the academic Left's flavor-of-the-week announced that Republican officeholders had been showering Betsey and me with patronage. He did not name the officeholders (who do not exist), much less the nature and the extent of the patronage. For myself, I do not recall knowing any Republican officeholders, and I certainly never received patronage of any kind. As for Betsey, if he meant President Bush, then how to explain the liberal Democrats in the Georgia State Senate? The feminists' "did-you-know" and "everyone knows" went on and on. Betsey and I could not stand each other. We fought like cats and dogs. And oh, Betsey made Gene so unhappy that he became an alcoholic. It may be asked: How can people expect to get away with such transparent mendacity? Rudyard Kipling bared the essentials in *The Jungle Book*, along with the essentials of "participatory democracy." The Bandar-Log (monkey-people) of central India gathered in a convention at which they chanted: "We are great. We are free. We are wonderful. We are the most wonderful people in all the jungle. We all say so, and so it must be true."

Occasionally, friends asked Betsey if she planned to reply to these and other slanders. "Good grief, no. I have work to do and don't have time to play in their sandbox." At confession, I asked Father Lopez if Jesus would forgive me if I killed the people who were pouring filth over her. He knew I was kidding, and we laughed. (Yes, even at confession, Catholic priests and communicants are allowed to wisecrack.) He reminded me of the prayer that Jesus taught us—the prayer I recite every night: "Forgive us our trespasses as we forgive those who trespass against us." Father Lopez offered a thought: "Gene, a man of your experience should know that people who tell such stories expose the desolation in their own marriages and love lives. Surely, such unhappy people need every prayer we can offer. For your penance, pray for them." For good measure, Betsey's response shamed me. She forgave her assailants at the moment she entered the Church—if not earlier. She, too, urged me to forgive, as I prayed to God to forgive my own sins. In this matter, as in others, she worried, above all, about my salvation. I am afraid that she had a lot to worry about.

As the campaign to destroy Betsey's career picked up momentum, our concern for each other mounted. We did not worry about lawsuits or threats to her academic position. We knew that no evidence existed to support her assailants' wild accusations of "gender discrimination"—in fact, the whole staff was female and loyal to Betsey. We knew she would prevail without difficulty. But I worried that Betsey, notwithstanding her notable strength, might get worn down, exacerbating the effects of her MS. She worried that I might act rashly, refusing her entreaties to remain silent and stay out of the fray. "It is my fight. Let me wage it according to my own lights." I gave her my word. We pledged that no matter how vicious the attacks on her, we would under no circumstances let them embitter us or corrode our life together. We refused to let events distract us from the work we had to do separately and in concert. Sicilians and the Georgians of the Caucasus say, "Revenge is a dish best eaten cold." In this respect Jews are smarter than Sicilians and Georgians: "The best revenge is to live well." We had each other, and we lived well. Still, every once in awhile Betsey found it necessary to remind her hot-tempered husband, "Vengeance is mine, sayeth the Lord."

Betsey believed in genuine "diversity." At the end of the 1980s, when she founded and directed the Women's Studies Program at Emory University, she wanted a variety of views—from left to right—represented in the program. She wanted students exposed to a wide range of views and to learn to defend their views firmly but to respect the views of others. I still recall the good feeling I had when Betsey hosted her first party at our home for the students and professors in the program. Feminists and antifeminists, radicals and conservatives, men and women, gays and straights mixed together easily, bantering, challenging, and teasing each other in a spirit of mutual respect and friendship. Betsey invited leading feminist scholars to Emory to see the program and exchange views. Hosts and guests showed each other courtesy and respect, and the students enjoyed a valuable experience.

There is a curious footnote to Betsey's insistence on an ideologically open women's studies program. Before Betsey's health deteriorated drastically, she lectured and participated in academic activities in Jamaica, Mexico, Ireland, France, Britain, and other countries. In 1990, speaking in French, Madame X (I no longer recall her name) of Ethiopia's national university invited her to Addis Ababa to offer advice on the introduction of women's studies. Betsey was puzzled. After all, the Ethiopians could have gone anywhere in the world for counsel. Betsey immediately accepted. I reminded her that a civil war was raging in Ethiopia, that the government's position had become precarious, and that she could find herself in mortal danger. She elected to go. She did not live recklessly, but neither did she live fearfully. I was worried about something else. A military *coup d'état* had brought a Marxist government to power, led by Mengistu Haile Mariam, a hard man even by Communist standards. Did the Ethiopians understand that Betsey was in bad odor with the American Left and that the radical feminists hated her? Did they understand that Betsey, although a Marxist, was firmly committed to intellectual freedom and ideological diversity? She received assurances that the Ethiopians knew precisely who she was. Why, then, did a Communist government choose her? We did not have the slightest idea but hoped to find out when we got there. We never got there. The regime fell and Mengistu went into exile. To my great relief, Betsey had to stay home.

In the 1990s, as Betsey's influence spread and the pro-life campaign waxed, the nastier radicals singled her out for all-out attack. The administration at Emory University fired a white low-level administrator in the Women's Studies Program who had been hired on a trial basis and found unsatisfactory. She filed suit. As every relevant administrator testified, Betsey had no authority in the matter and could not have fired her even if she had wanted to. The Emory administration made a technical error in the dating of her firing, so it settled with her before the matter went to trial. The complainant singled Betsey out for abuse with a string of unsubstantiated and absurd charges. Feminists and other radical leftists joined the attacks on Betsey without claiming to have evidence. They suggested that Betsey had been named in the final settlement. Not true. They suggested that Betsey had to pay part of the settlement. She did not—not a dime. She did not figure in the settlement at all. This is no "he said/ she said" matter. Everything at issue can be verified by independent research—something honest historians do.

When it looked as if the charges against Betsey would be heard in court, the African-Americans in Atlanta rallied to her *en masse*. She had the support of the women who worked for her in the women's studies office, the janitorial staff, her faculty colleagues, and business and trade-union women from the Atlanta community. Not one African-American in Atlanta—not one—offered to testify against her; a number volunteered to testify against those who were slandering her. The white radical feminists had to import an African-American from the Northeast to attack her. At that, the import did not publicly endorse any of the charges hurled at Betsey. Rather, she gave the radicals' game away by demanding to know how a liberal university like Emory could tolerate the author of *Feminism Is Not the Story of My Life* on its faculty.

Matters did not end there. The *Journal of American History* published an interview with a left-wing historian who declared that Betsey and I had joined the extreme Right and even become leaders. The interviewer and the editor of the *JAH* published that and other accusations without pretense of having sought evidence or checked the purported facts. Betsey spoke and wrote for the Right-to-Life Movement and lent her name to a few Republican Party functions. That was the extent of her political activity. Apart from other considerations, her physical disabilities would have prevented her doing more, even if she had wanted to. For myself, apart from offering political opinions in an occasional essay or book review, I had refrained from political activity for some twenty years. I have no idea what movement I was supposed to have joined or supported, much less led. And I know of no movement that has counted me among its number. Neither the author, nor his interviewer, nor the *JAH*'s editor made an effort to support the allegations or gave any indication that he had bothered to check the facts. The well-known historians who constituted the *JAH*'s editorial board did not comment on, much less protest, the gross violation of professional ethics and common decency.

No matter how vicious the slander or flagrant the libel, Betsey had no recourse at law. As a "public personality," she was fair game and could not sue. Probably she would not have sued even if she could have. A strong advocate of tort reform, she had an aversion to litigation. And she detested public brawls.

The increasingly obscene attacks reached their low point in Betsey's last years. As her health was collapsing, one of the radical Left's less talented propagandists set a new low. Protesting a cover-up, he wrote that the charges against Betsey had never been properly investigated. When President Bush appointed Betsey to the NEH Governing Council, she underwent an exhaustive three-month investigation by the FBI. Nothing unusual there: All appointees face the same grueling review. The FBI gave her a clean bill of health. It is no secret that Democratic as well as Republican senators review NEH appointments carefully and that the leading authority for the Democrats is Senator Edward M. Kennedy of Massachusetts. Betsey sailed through. Several of the radical Left's academic stars endorsed the attacks on Betsey in full knowledge that the accusation of a cover-up was false. One of the more despicable had been appointed to the NEH Governing Council by President Clinton and knew the drill from personal experience.

Betsey treated these gambits with contempt, but she had a harder time with the betrayals of old friends. The behavior of leading figures in the Ivy League and elsewhere stung her. The feminists' attacks mounted as MS disabled her. Celebrated scholars, long on record for praising her scholarship and moral fiber, quietly severed relations with her. Well before the last decade of her life they systematically excluded her from the academic programs and conferences they sponsored in her subjects of expertise. In effect, they lent tacit support to the radicals' effort to turn her into a nonperson or to destroy her career altogether. Simultaneously, they publicly associated with some of the worst of her assailants without even pretending to believe their charges against Betsey. I seethed. Betsey winced. These were people she had every reason to believe would stand by her or at least do nothing to hurt her. She swallowed hard, refusing to let hurt feelings poison her. Her entrance into the Church strengthened but did not create her forbearance and willingness to forgive. She could be hurt badly but had no capacity for vengeance or hatred. Her friends knew as much. After her death, one of her colleagues wrote me, speaking for others: "I was always struck by the fact that she did not hate her enemies." I doubt that Betsey ever hated anyone, and in all our years together I never saw her willfully hurt another human being. She stood on James 1:20: "The wrath of man worketh not the righteousness of God." When her husband's anger at the viciousness of her detractors welled up, she told him to hush up and pray for the salvation of their immortal souls.

5

Pain

Dime como mueres, y te diré quien eres.
[Tell me how you die, and I shall tell you who you are.]

—Octavio Paz

I never quite knew how Betsey saw herself when she looked in a mirror. She did not stop traffic or turn every head when she crossed a street or entered a restaurant, but she knew—as did her husband—that a great many men thought her lovely. I once mentioned a young woman whom I had known years before. Uncommonly intelligent and appealing but without strikingly good looks, she well described herself as "an OK-looking girl." Betsey found the story charming and seemed to feel that way about herself. I surmised that she thought herself attractive enough to feel relaxed with the looks God gave her and to have no need for a man who found her wanting. She never displayed the slightest desire to compete with other women and gave no hint of seeing herself as lovely or even particularly pretty. Every day I told her (at least once) what I believed—that she was beautiful. She purred but, clearly, took my words as a loving husband's star-gazing. Her self-effacement was all well and good, but I loved to look at her, the more so with every passing year. Beauty, we have been told, is in the eye of the beholder. For this beholder, she was the personification of elegance, poise, grace, and dignity. She stood tall, slender, pleasingly proportioned, and with shapely legs. Her smile enhanced silken skin, high cheekbones, and dark brown eyes.

I recall only one occasion when Betsey showed frustration about her physical appearance. Despite unfeigned modesty and lifelong observance of "play the cards you're dealt," she had a bad moment with the onset of MS. When she lost control of her right leg, she had to wear a heavy, unsightly brace that, even with my assistance, she struggled to put on and take off. She had to replace her tastefully selected shoes with bulky white sneakers and give up skirts and dresses for pants. One day her eyes filled with tears she fought to hold back. I tried to soothe her by assuring her that pants showed off her sexy rear end better than skirts and dresses. She kissed me for the thought but grimaced.

She recovered quickly from her bad moment, steeling herself to rely on a cane, then a crutch, then two crutches, then a walker, and finally a wheelchair. Until the last six months or so of her life, she continued to edit a historical journal, drive her car, write articles, meet classes, remain available to her students, and work with me on a book on proslavery ideology. I tried to rein her in, to reason with her, to get her to take a more realistic view of her condition. She said all the right things and, continuing to drive herself, did as she pleased. Taking care of people was high on her agenda; taking care of herself somehow got lost in the shuffle. On one matter I put my foot down. I had always done the preliminary work: the chopping, slicing, and sautéing of onions, mushrooms, and other vegetables; accordingly, I maintained that her reputation as a superior cook rested entirely on my extraordinary ability to peel, chop, slice, and sauté. But at a certain point I refused to let her stand or even sit in front of a stove. I took over most of the cooking, and we dined out a lot. I am a fair cook, so we did all right. With due modesty, I claim the right to crow about my Italian meatballs, tomato sauces, lasagna, and veal cutlets. But the days of savoring her lobster risotto, *boeuf bourguignon*, paella, *vitello tonnato*, veal and artichokes in cream sauce, and imaginative fish, seafood, chicken, and pasta dishes were over.

Learning from the Misfortune of Others

From François La Rochefoucauld onward, it has been observed that most people bear with equanimity the misfortune of others. Not Betsey. She never felt sorry for herself in no small part because she put her terrible afflictions in perspective. She read widely and traveled enough to know a good deal about the plight of people all over the world. She drew strength and courage from them. In her twenties, working for a domestic antipoverty program, she got a firsthand look at inner-city suffering, the depths of which she had not previously encountered. The condition of the poor in several countries she visited sickened her. Her knowledge of German served her well in the days of the Berlin Wall, when she took care of East German refugees. Their courage made a lasting impression. And at home in later years, she comforted her beloved father during his slow, tortured deterioration from Parkinson's disease and other infirmities.

After my mother died, Betsey pleaded with my father to come to Rochester to live with us. He refused. The old curmudgeon cherished her but had long ago resolved not to burden his children as his family had burdened him. By the time he turned ninety he had become a danger to himself and others. At that point we refused to take "no" for an answer. He came, and we provided a part-time nurse and companion. In a year or so he fell desperately ill. The doctor and nurse gave up on him, certain that he would not last another twenty-four hours. Betsey would have none of it: "That cantankerous old man will die when he is ready, and not one minute before, and he is not going to die in my house without a fight." She thereupon asked what kind of food might keep him going awhile. They pointed out that he would not take food and that it would be fatal to move him to a hospital to be fed intravenously. He was dying and probably would not survive more than a day or so. Betsey uttered "uh-huh"—which told me that she did not believe a word and intended to do as she saw fit. She asked them for a list of appropriate foods, dismissed them with thanks, and went shopping. When she returned, she disappeared into the kitchen and came out with a concoction that resembled a milkshake. My father was barely conscious but just enough to return some of her smiles. She sat with him all night and into the morning—rubbing his hands, talking to him even when he probably could not hear her, and spoon-feeding him whenever he was alert enough to take a sip. I was sure he would die at any minute, and, I am embarrassed to say, I pretty well froze. At a certain point, she told me that I needed to get some sleep—her gentle way of telling me to get out of her way. Within two days my father recovered. The doctor and nurse could not believe their eyes. The doctor said he would write an account for the *New England Journal of Medicine,* were it not that it might make him look incompetent. "Your wife saved your father's life. I don't believe in miracles, but I just saw one."

In 1980, when I turned fifty, I came down with a heart condition that in time proved minor but seemed dangerous at the time. I had to take a medical leave from the University of Rochester and could not travel or do much of anything. The medication made it impossible for me to work, and I spent each day reading the sports pages and a chapter or two of Henry Kissinger's two-volume *Memoirs*—worth reading for many reasons, including hilarious descriptions of the social scene in Washington. For the better part of a year I was a basket case, without energy for much of anything. There was Betsey: a loving, attentive, upbeat nurse. Neither a word nor a gesture of complaint. My infirmity undoubtedly bore hard on her, but she never showed it. She had not yet fallen prey to MS, but she had assorted lesser physical problems. Her quiet refusal to feel sorry for herself under any circumstances vitiated any tendency I may have had to indulge in self-pity. Throughout our marriage, I had her example before me. A decade or so later, Betsey and I were having lunch at a pleasant café in Atlanta's Neiman Marcus department store. My right leg started to freeze. I thought it was "asleep." Despite my rubbing, it got worse and spread to my arm. Suddenly I pitched forward. Betsey dropped some money on the table and got me to the garage. A stranger helped to get me into her car. She sped across town to Emory's medical center. Although neither of us had ever had a stroke, we both knew what was happening. She had no intention of negotiating with the staff at Emory Hospital's emergency room—a fine staff, by the way. Instead she took me to Emory Clinic, where our doctor had his office. She settled me on a bench and disappeared momentarily. Betsey did not ask for help, knowing how much time might be consumed. Instead, she purloined a wheelchair and took me straight to our doctor's office. She did not ask if our doctor was available. She informed the nurse that she was sure he would be.

While Dr. David Roberts was examining me, Betsey and I talked about the major-league-baseball pennant races. She later assured me that I had been coherent. There was one trouble. I had not been thinking about baseball but about a paper I had been writing. The words that came out of my mouth had nothing to do with the words I was thinking and trying to speak. Dr. Roberts then had me strapped to something or other, assuring me that the chances of the clot's dissolving before it hit my brain were good. I asked what would happen if it did hit my brain. He replied: "Then you're in big trouble." The treatment worked, and the threat passed quickly. I got off lightly.

The prospect of hanging, Samuel Johnson observed in defense of capital punishment, concentrates the mind wonderfully. So, I might add, does the prospect of becoming paralyzed and badly crippled. I was terrified that the paralysis of my right side would render me permanently immobile and scramble my brain, spelling the end of my work life. Mostly, I choked on the thought of becoming a horrible burden on Betsey. Death confronts most people with their greatest terror, but fear of death has never plagued me. In 1957, as I went into an operating room, I heard the surgeon tell my doctor that my condition was much worse than previously thought and that the chances for my survival were so-so. In the operating room I looked around, thinking that I might not come off the table alive. I was resigned, not frightened. I do not assert the absurdity that I have no terrors of my own, only that they have never included death. In the 1960s I lived with constant death threats and lost no sleep. About death I have always been fatalistic, and I expect to "go gentle into that good night." But the thought that I might become a crushing burden on Betsey terrified me. I knew precisely how she would react. "In sickness and in health, till death do us part." She would have taken care of me no matter how great the sacrifice and cost to herself. She would have suffered through all the years it took. And she would have done it as lovingly and cheerfully as humanly possible. The knowledge that she would remain rock-solid dismayed rather than comforted me. I did not know how I could live with the burden placed on her.

Sometime after the onset of Betsey's MS, we spent a week at the Huega Center in Salt Lake City, which brings together groups of fifty—twenty-five MS patients and twenty-five "significant others." When we arrived, we learned that in cases in which one spouse comes down with MS, the divorce rate is 80 percent. At first, we found it incomprehensible; by the time we left the center, we understood. Many people with MS undergo destructive personality changes that make life impossible for those around them. Even Betsey showed a slight

118

diminution of her extraordinary patience and good cheer. It was no small comfort for both of us that we would survive together no matter what happened. We had no doubt that we would remain among the 20 percent.

Activities at the Huega Center consisted of daily physical therapy, lectures, and group sessions for the patients with separate group sessions for the others. Betsey was grateful for the opportunity and found the week useful in various ways. I and those like me got a first-rate crash course in caring for MS patients and for coping with sundry responsibilities. Together, Betsey and I learned important things. Many of the patients seemed in much worse shape than Betsey. Some— maybe most—had tension-ridden relations with their partners. The suffering we witnessed took a toll on us, modified by recognition of the love and courage that her fellow patients and their partners displayed. The experience reinforced Betsey's always-present awareness of people much less fortunate than herself and strengthened her prayers of gratitude to God.

Frightening Incidents

In Betsey's last year or two she had four frightening incidents, which, as usual, she took in stride and I did not. Our home has three floors. You enter on the middle floor, not the first. Her study was on the third floor with our bedroom and guest room. Above all, she wanted maximum sunlight; the room she selected was the brightest in the house. My study was an extraordinarily large room on the lowest floor. Any scholar might envy it if he did not mind a total lack of sunlight. James Crawford was working for us on a day in which she collapsed in the shower. He came down to tell me that the shower had been running for an uncommonly long time. I rushed upstairs and found her crumbled on the floor of the shower stall. Fortunately, she was unhurt. Since I did not have the strength to lift her, I wrapped her in a bath towel and called for James. She snapped out of it without serious repercussions. But from that point on, we agreed that I had to be there whenever she showered or bathed. We put a chair and special rods in the shower for her. She loved her baths, and our Jacuzzi did her good. But her quickening physical decline made bathing difficult. I helped her in and out of the tub, but it was not easy. I accompanied her to make sure nothing untoward happened. But it got harder and harder for her.

Sometime later she stepped out of the shower and pitched forward. If I had not been there to catch her, she would have gone head-down on the bathroom tile. James was not working that day, and I had difficulty lifting her into a chair placed between the shower and the bathtub. She remained unconscious and could not control her body. I tried to revive her but without success. I could not call 911 immediately. I had no phone within reach and dared not leave her, lest she fall again. I no longer had the strength to carry her, but I finally managed to get her into the bedroom and lay her on our bed. I called our friend Tina Trent, who proved heroic then and in the months ahead. She came immediately, and we got Betsey to the hospital. Tina, Betsey's graduate student, shortly thereafter got her Ph.D. She had served as spokeswoman for the pro-choice movement in Atlanta and worked in Democratic Party political campaigns. Many, probably most, of Betsey's graduate students were leftists who disagreed with her politics but valued her professional training. Tina had also worked at a number of jobs, including construction. Not surprisingly, she is a good deal stronger than I and handled Betsey as I no longer had the strength to.

After Betsey came home, she had an automobile accident. An excellent driver with superior reflexes, she always kept her mind on the road, knowing that others did not drive as well as she and that she had to exercise maximum caution. She never had accidents. Coming home from Emory one day, she passed out just as she approached our home, knocking over our neighbors' brick mailbox and cutting it in half. Thank God, their children were not playing there, as they often did. Her doctor thereupon grounded her.

Some time afterwards we went to Augusta for a meeting of the St. George Tucker Society. We were to appear at a session to discuss our book *The Mind of the Master Class*. As we walked from our motel to the meeting center, she collapsed. Friends and people on the motel's staff got her back to our room, and I called 911. By the time the paramedics arrived, she had come to. She adamantly refused to be taken to the hospital, announcing that it was nothing, and that she would be fine. She added that her husband was prone to panic and should be ignored. I had indeed been known to panic—whenever I feared for my wife. I insisted that the paramedics take her to the emergency room. They said that Georgia law forbade them to do so without her consent. I bellowed that her husband was giving consent. They patiently explained that under the law her husband did not count. (Despite my bellowing, it is a good law.) The chief paramedic appreciated the seriousness of her illness and called me aside. He told me to let her sleep for two hours and then wake her. If she was incoherent or not functioning properly, I was to call him immediately. Under those circumstances I could legally make the decision for her. Two hours later I woke her—more or less. She was incoherent. I asked if she knew me. Of course she did. I was Ed (her father); then I became Ed (her brother). I asked where she was. She replied that she was at home in Atlanta with her husband. Who is your husband? Gene. And who am I? You're Ed. I called the paramedics.

Each episode had the same general cause. Betsey had to take a variety of medicines for her MS; rheumatic arthritis; back, leg, hip, and knee pains; bladder infections; and sinus headaches. She had a battery of fine doctors, but sometimes their medicines interacted badly.

Never-Ending Illnesses

As Betsey grew older, she had to contend with rheumatoid arthritis. I knew just enough to think that it reinforced the effects of the MS, intensifying her pain and crippling her further. "Just enough" proved not nearly enough. As usual, she hid from me as much as she could. I saw her knees, feet, and "good leg" as well as "bad leg" frequently swollen and obviously causing considerable pain. Still, I underestimated the extent of her distress, apart from that caused by her other medical problems, until I overheard her conversation with a young neighbor, who also suffered from rheumatoid arthritis. The ladies exchanged accounts of their difficulties, and only then did I recognize the degree of pain it discretely caused. Far from being an exacerbation of Betsey's MS and spinal condition, it was a dreadful blow all its own.

Pinched nerves put her fortitude to another severe test. Never having had a pinched nerve, I had little sense of the terrible pain that it caused. A number of acquaintances filled me in, describing the pain as unbearable, and I started to recognize the extent of Betsey's agony. When the pain became intolerable even to her stoical self, she had an epidural, which once or twice helped a lot, more often a little. I do not remember how many times she went to Emory Clinic for epidurals that yielded so-so results. I do remember her gratitude for the degree of relief she got.

As if that were not enough, she lived with severe allergies. Atlanta has good weather, although many natives do not appreciate it. Winters are mild and short. Summers can be hot and humid but are also short, and temperatures usually drop significantly at night. For most of the year Atlanta bathes in a lengthy and lovely spring and fall. Besides, Atlantans who gripe at the humidity might try a summer in any port city. Boston, New York, and Washington are much worse; New Orleans and Houston are not to be borne. Unfortunately,

Atlanta is overridden with pollen, so woe unto those who suffer from allergies. Betsey coped with severe headaches, but, as her health deteriorated, she had increasing difficulty.

Along the way, Betsey had serious trouble with her teeth. Her front teeth were crooked and, in consequence, she had a bad bite that hurt her in a variety of ways. When she turned forty, our dentist in upstate New York suggested that she have all her teeth pulled. Always ready to face what she had to without groans, she was ready to consider it, but wanted a second opinion. She saw another dentist who saved her teeth. But she still had a bad bite that caused soreness and threatened to require stern measures. She frequently ground her teeth when asleep, sometimes so severely that she woke me. For years she had had to cope with one more ache. The best I could do was to put my hand between her lower and upper teeth to stop the grinding. In Atlanta, we signed on with a prestigious dental firm. Dr. David Garber, our dentist, recommended a brace and surgery to straighten her front teeth. A woman in her fifties, she bore that unattractive brace without complaint for about a year and had the surgery. Dr. Salama, the surgeon, did a wonderful job. I was grateful to him and relieved for her. But in truth, I was not entirely pleased. I had always found her crooked teeth alluring.

Betsey had an extraordinary ability to endure pain. For decades she endured pains, the cumulative effect of which would have overwhelmed most people. She took her lesser aches and pains in stride, but they generally came when she was bedeviled by the more serious ailments, among which were frequent bladder infections, sometimes light, sometimes acute. When an infection did not intersect with other sources of pain, she bore it as just one more unpleasantness. I watched her carefully but sometimes did not pick up the extent of her distress. In her last year, hazardous infections became worse and more frequent. She had to be catheterized in the hospital and to catheterize herself at home. The procedure proved difficult and hurtful, especially when she had to do it herself. Catch-22: Catherization was supposed to prevent infection, but the difficulty of inserting the catheter included irritations that created their own danger of infection. Toward the end, her bladder became badly infected along with much of her body.

A Hard Last Year

Mary Odem, Betsey's colleague in the Departments of History and Women's Studies, told a story at Emory's memorial meeting, which she planned and directed flawlessly:

> I want to close by recounting my last encounter with Betsey, which made a powerful and I think lasting impression on me. I visited Betsey in the hospital in mid-December, a time when she was very weak. When I walked into the room, she once again was very gracious as she welcomed me and sought to make me feel comfortable. She talked with appreciation and respect about the personnel who were caring for her, and she seemed to know them all by name. At the time a young nurse, recently graduated, was caring for Betsey, and struggling with a certain procedure and taking a long time to complete it. Though Betsey was clearly in discomfort and pain, she spoke only encouraging words to the young nurse: "Don't worry, you can do it; you're doing a wonderful job."

Mary added, "She was a dedicated teacher. Her example of dignity, compassion, and commitment in the face of suffering and pain will stay with me." And at that, Mary may not have known what Betsey was up to in that hospital. Betsey was carefully reading and criticizing the final draft of Sheila O'Connor-Ambrose's doctoral dissertation.

Betsey kept her promise to Jesus to help others with her last breath. She had borne up well under the MS. She injected herself with Betaseron every other day and submitted to a rigorous regimen of physical therapy, which took a big bite out of her day. The physical therapy included frequent time-consuming trips to Atlanta's Shepherd Center, which treats patients with MS and spinal disorders, and to a nearby athletic club. Even more consuming was her daily physical therapy at home. She rode a stationary bicycle; did good deal of stretching on a mat; balanced herself on contraptions designed to strengthen her legs; and engaged in assorted exercises. All in all, she spent hours each day just to stay steady and resist deterioration. Her physical strength and endurance astonished me. Despite my aversion to exercise, I tried hers, usually succumbing to exhaustion in ten minutes.

At home, it sometimes seemed that Betsey found time for everything. Even she could not manage that miracle, but she came close. She wanted to say the rosary, but when, in her incredibly crowded day, was she supposed to find time? Easy: She said her rosary while bicycling late in the evening as part of her daily physical therapy. And before turning in at night, no matter how exhausted or hurting, she read from the Gospels (her favorite was St. John) or the *Catechism*, or the *Magnificat*, or an encyclical, or something from one of her beloved Saint Theresas. What I could not figure out was how she found time to read *Harry Potter* and the flow of mystery novels that gave her much pleasure. In 1998 she published a piece in *Books and Culture* on one of her favorites: "Of Sin and Horses: Dick Francis's 10-lb Penalty." She kept reading mystery novels right up to her final trip to the hospital.

For some years the MS remained level and the prognosis good. She was doing fine, but at a price. Betsey knew a good deal about medicine; I did not. But when her health deteriorated in her last few years, I did not doubt that her body had been taking a bad beating.

Another Catch-22. When her chronic back condition got worse—much worse—she had to curtail the physical therapy she needed to contain the MS. Her legs weakened perceptively, the good one as well as the afflicted. Having to curtail physical therapy rendered her more likely to fall. Some falls were serious, some not. Falls at home alarmed me; falls in concrete parking lots gave me fits. On one occasion she had a terrible fall on the tile floor of a department store, badly hurting her knee. Weeks of intense pain ensued, worsening her already greatly reduced mobility. On another, she collapsed as we were leaving a restaurant and required CPR, which left her in pain for weeks. At home I had to watch her closely because she was less than forthcoming. She responded to falls that hurt her in the same way that she responded to those that did not: "Stop fussing. I'm all right." Some of her most alarming falls came during the night when she got out of bed to go to the bathroom. We kept a light on to reduce the chances of her losing her balance, but her difficulties increased as her body weakened. I pleaded that she wake me whenever she had to get up, but she refused to disturb my sleep. One night she had a bad fall, which awakened me. This time, hurt badly, she did not try to disguise the severity. Reluctantly, she agreed to wake me in the future. She did so, and we further eased the problem by putting a commode next to her bedside.

In her last few years the pain she had long borne grew steadily more intense, spinning out of control in her last year. I cannot begin to describe her mounting torment. Her private notebooks for June 2006 record one of her worst periods. Noting worse pain than usual, she was upset with herself. She just was not getting enough done, and her desk was piled with unfinished business. "But I don't want to kid myself. When the pain is bad, it is fierce."

When we awoke in the morning, I did not ask, "Are you in pain?" But, rather: "How bad is it? And where is it particularly bad this morning?" Toward the end, on the worst days, she could not help crying out—something she had never done. Her back pains reached a point at which she could not reach back, and I had to hook her bra. She had a good laugh when I remarked that before the sexual revolution, boys had to sweat just to be able to feel a girl's breasts. If a girl wanted to "pet," convention required that she ask you to desist while she squirmed into a position to make sure you proceeded. Every boy, I explained, learned how to hold a girl firmly with one hand and unhook her bra with the other. It was an art. Boys learned how to unhook a bra—but not how to hook it. And sure enough, to Betsey's amusement, I had trouble hooking hers. The amusement dwindled, as her body ached more and more. Yet somehow she managed to smile—never missing a day. Her smiles came naturally, but also from her knowledge of how much they meant to her husband.

Betsey had always arisen at six a.m. and worked until late in the evening. When we married, I found hard to believe that I was living with a woman who worked longer hours than I. Under the circumstances, the necessity to reduce drastically her schedule tormented her. After she entered the Church, she went to an early morning daily Mass as often as possible—that is, on days on which she was not due at the university. The decline in her health compelled her to give up daily Mass and Sunday's Perpetual Adoration. Betsey considered daily Mass and the Sunday vigil sources of strength, and she fretted over having to desist. From her private notebook, October 9, 2002: "Sins of omission: I am behind on everything. No daily Mass right now. I miss it—especially since the loss seems to diminish my prayer life." April 6, 2003, at Adoration: "Fr. Lopez says that my pain is my penance, and there has been enough of that—worse than usual, and I am not sure why. And so much to do—But I have not had a true retreat, have not really given myself over to contemplation & worship. I keep searching for true holiness, charity, self-denial, and I fall woefully short."

"Whatever fools may say," C. S. Lewis observed in A Grief Observed, "the body can suffer twenty times more than the mind. The mind has always some power of evasion. At worst, the unbearable thought only comes back and back, but the physical pain can be absolutely continuous." I knew that Betsey had reached the end of her tether when she agreed to retire the next year. Worried about her health, I had long urged her to consider retirement at sixty-five or earlier. She would not consider it. Her love for teaching and for her students compelled her to continue as long as she could. So when she changed her mind, I knew that she was finally taking the measure of her condition. At that point, we began to talk about our future. We planned to take more frequent and longer weekends at Château Élan in north Georgia, which we had long substituted for summer vacations of a week or two. Mostly, there were little things. True to my rejection of exercise, I never took walks and, needless to say, considered joggers akin to lunatics. But when we got Josef, Betsey and I sometimes walked him together and much enjoyed it. Almost everything I did with Betsy gave me pleasure. But just as we were starting to enjoy walks together, she lost control of her leg. Then, as she made valiant efforts to adjust to her greatly weakened health, we looked forward to having me wheel her around the circle on which we lived. Other little things promised happy moments for us. None came to be.

For years Betsey struggled with chronic back pains but nothing like those of her last year or two. She was diagnosed with stenosis, which accounted for the brutal pain that moved from hips to knees to legs to feet. She needed a spinal operation. One more Catch-22. Her first-rate surgeon, as well as our trusted Dr. Roberts, and we ourselves all wanted to wait a few months to allow her to build up her bodily strength to face the pressure. But Betsey could not wait. The increasing intensity of the pain overwhelmed her. Notwithstanding her almost superhuman ability to suffer intense pain, she could go no further. The operation lasted eight-and-a-half hours. Our surgeon accomplished all we could have hoped for, but the operation placed new and heavy strains on her body, as we all had feared it might. When she returned after three weeks in the hospital and rehabilitation center, I often had to lift her out of bed and into a wheelchair to get her to the bathroom. I then helped her to shower or bathe and dress. She had to be touched or moved with the utmost care, lest she be hurt and badly bruised. Her morning routine had proceeded slowly long before the operation; afterwards, it proceeded at a snail's pace. All in all, it took two to three hours, during every minute of which she suffered, sometimes dreadfully, although she did her best not to let on.

When Betsey came out of the rehabilitation center, we hoped for the best. In a few days she collapsed. This time she succumbed to rampant diarrhea, which lasted for a couple of days before I could persuade her to return to the hospital. At the hospital she was diagnosed with colitis. She was badly dehydrated again, and her bladder problems worsened. After another three weeks of treatment and rehabilitation, she was discharged just before Christmas. I was ecstatic at being able to take care of her at home and spend the holidays with her. But her frailty raised a red flag, and I was fearful. Her brother joined us for the holidays, and we had an excellent Christmas Eve dinner—I seem to recall that we all had trout—at a fine nearby restaurant. On Christmas Day I made filet mignon in butter and wine sauce in the French manner, gritting my teeth to make hers well-done. She insisted on caramelizing the shallots, which she did quickly without putting undue pressure on herself. I served a particularly good Château Neuf du Pape, her favorite wine with filet mignon. Betsey was overjoyed with having had a lovely holiday weekend. She poured out gratitude to God. That was fine and appropriate. And she poured out gratitude to her husband for taking such good care of her. That was neither fine nor appropriate, but it was vintage Betsey. She always valued—far above and beyond anything called for—whatever anyone did for her.

She seemed happier and more relaxed than I had seen her in a long time. Her brother and I worried about her frailty and unsteadiness but hoped the worst was over. After a couple of dreadful nights, she collapsed again. As intransigent as ever, she spoke sharply: "If you take me back to the hospital, I shall never forgive you." She had never spoken to me like that, and it cut to the quick. She later apologized and agreed to return to the hospital. In retrospect, I wonder if she had a premonition that if she went back, she would not return.

The New Year's holiday was an inversion of the Christmas holiday. Early in our marriage we attended some New Year's Eve parties but discovered to our mutual relief that they were not to our taste. We also found that we did not like to eat out on New Year's Eve. Not even at our favorite restaurants: too noisy, too hurried, nothing quite up to snuff. (Recall the words of that great Italian-American philosopher, Yogi Berra: "Nobody goes to that restaurant anymore; it's too crowded.") Year after year we turned New Year's into a quietly lovely occasion at home. We enjoyed a singular dinner for which we did not spare the expense. It began with Caspian caviar and champagne. Then came Betsey's not-to-be-believed turkey tetrazzini or fettuccine alfredo with truffles and a Caesar salad. More often than not I served Amarone or an attractive alternative. We ended with espresso and one of her creative desserts. Year after year, our quiet New Year's Eves brightened the holiday season.

On December 31, 2006, we had a different kind of quiet New Year's Eve. Betsey was back in the hospital—in agony. Two days later she died.

Reduced to skin and bones, she bruised badly at the slightest touch. Her stomach distended, she looked as if she were well along in pregnancy. Her breasts and much of her body had withered, her hands gnarled. I desperately wanted to hold her, and she asked me to. But the gentlest of touches hurt her. Infection spread everywhere: bladder, kidneys, colon, and, finally, bloodstream. The doctors were puzzled to find that her white blood count soared to a level three times the normal—a level only seen in leukemia patients. It resisted treatment, as did the dehydration and everything else. Her body shut down.

Betsey held on against all odds. The doctors, having expected her to die a day or two before she did, shook their heads at her extraordinary willpower. Her family and friends were not surprised. Until the end, her willpower—her tenacious love of life—identified her as the woman she was.

6

Time Does Not Heal All Things

Began day with hope & joy—or happiness. Prayed & then exercised and thought through all the things I need to do. By the time I was getting dressed, my mood had suddenly turned to sorrow—I think because of the recognition of how little I actually can do. I move so slowly. Everything requires more energy, and I am so slow to recognize my own limitations. . . .

I found myself praying—at my little altar—Dear Lord, let my pain and suffering be of some use to some one.

—Elizabeth Fox-Genovese,
private notebook, January 9, 2004

Betsey's reserve and carriage cloaked an extraordinary zest for life. Cheerful and energetic, she kept our home awash in smiles and laughter. She took the utmost pleasure in our dogs and cats, in the many plants she adorned every room with, and in the flowers I brought her every week. In 1986 she wrote in her diary: "I enjoy my life. It seems right, seems for real as they say." Joseph Bottum, in an obituary, recalled his last sight of Betsey at an editorial board meeting of the journal *First Things:* "Watching her hobble on her awkward crutches, I thought how sad she must be to suffer so. But the sadness was mine, not hers. She seemed, somehow, to have grown wiser and braver as her illness advanced. Grander, happier, greater." Some months af-

Late 1990s Atlanta

ter she died, Nancy Wilson, her oldest and dearest friend and confidante, wrote to me:

She was, as you know, a deeply happy woman. Even, perhaps especially (despite pain and loss of mobility) in the past fifteen years or so. I think in those years she laughed more—wonderful warm laughter— than she had in all the years I'd known her. She had moments of grief, yes, for what she could no longer do, but far more moments of joy. Her faith was part of that, I know, but the part we talked about more was her life with you.

Our life together brought us inexpressible joy. Her high spirits swept me along and (almost) overcame the gloominess that has dogged me since childhood. Yet, Betsey also lived in accordance with John Randolph of Roanoke's *bon mot*: "Life is not so important as the duties of life." Paradoxically, that, too, underscored her zest for life.

I have no idea what I would have done on the day Betsey died, were it not for Rebecca, Ed, Nancy, and the dear friends who rallied around. Betsey's love of family manifested itself as big sister to Ed and as second mother to Rebecca, who was seven years her junior. By their own accounts she made a huge difference in their rearing.

Betsey, Rebecca, and Ed had some tense moments from time to time, as all siblings do, but their love and support for each other shone through. It was my privilege to have observed it.

All in all, Betsey spent seven of her last nine-and-a-half weeks in the hospital or rehabilitation center. Shortly after she returned to Emory Hospital for the third time, I received a phone call in the middle of the night. The doctor on duty told me that Betsey was being moved to the intensive care unit. She said little else. When I got to the hospital, I asked the doctor to speak frankly. She replied quietly, "The family should be prepared." In the intensive care unit, Betsey lay unconscious: shriveled, writhing, wincing, contorted. It was more than I could bear. The next morning, although she did not awaken, she seemed more comfortable, but it was about over. Within a few hours she died, lying straight back, serene, once more radiating beauty. I thank God for that last sight of her at peace. That day, although hideous, was not the worst of my life. I was numb. The worst day of my life—the day I lost it—came when I awoke on the morning of her cremation, visualizing her going into that oven. Betsey and I had chosen cremation early in our marriage, thinking to blend our ashes in a single urn. In our parlor, her ashes occupy an urn large enough to receive mine, awaiting our joint burial in consecrated ground.

We have all heard people ask incredulously: How can a marriage hold up for decades? Doesn't the fire go out? You "love" your spouse, but are you really still "in love" with her? Don't you get weary of spending every day with the same person, year after year? I wish I knew what planet these people come from. I have been told of the deadening pressures on married couples by the constant chores of rearing children while struggling to survive in a competitive economy and make ends meet. Not having had children, I have no grounds on which to judge, but I do have friends and acquaintances who face those problems with every appearance of growing closer year by year. For myself, all I can say with certainty is that I loved—and love—Betsey more with every passing year and have no doubt that she loved me even more at the end than at the beginning. If love cannot grow stronger over time—if it must recede or go stale—what is life worth?

Where do we turn for consolation? To Plato or Aristotle? To Cicero or Seneca? To the *Consolation of Philosophy* by the Christian martyr Boethius? Throughout history, the greatest minds have pointed us toward philosophy. The philosopher Ann Hartle—Betsey's colleague and friend—has written in *Death and the Disinterested Spectator*: "Those who must escape the despair of modern philosophy, find themselves returning to the beginning as if to home. There, philosophy is allotted her sublimer task, preparation for death. But for this task, she needs her own muses. Philosophy herself cannot console." Surely, the muses to which Ann Hartle refers consist, first and foremost, of faith. And yet, is even faith enough? Is anything enough? Monsignor Richard Lopez told a story in his sermon at Betsey's funeral Mass: "I recall when I was a seminarian at work in a hospital, a twenty-year-old died unexpectedly on the operating table. A kindly priest came in to comfort the mother with the hope of Resurrection. I will never forget her words: 'With the Resurrection, I have my faith, but what, Father, do I do with this pain in my heart?'"

Notwithstanding philosophy and faith, ratiocination and the heart that has its reasons, it does no good to hear well-meaning brothers and sisters in Christ tell me that Betsey is with God in a better place. C. S. Lewis remarked when kind friends tried to assure him that his deceased wife was with God: "In one sense that is most certain. She is, like God, incomprehensible and unimaginable."

Before I returned to the Church after fifty years in the wilderness, I asked myself if I could believe in an afterlife. Jesus promises everlasting life, and I believe Him. What everlasting life means I have no idea. At the risk of contradicting these words, I pray that Betsey and I will be blended spiritually, much as our ashes will be blended in that urn. We are told that in Heaven we shall see the face of God. If allowed to enter Heaven, I shall see Him in her smile.

I think back on our improbable blind date as the day the Holy Ghost pronounced my sinful soul worth saving. Betsey was His gift to me—by far the greatest gift I ever received. In the fourth year of our marriage, I dedicated my book, *Roll, Jordan Roll: The World the Slaves Made*: "For Miss Betsey, My Own Personal Bright and Morning Star." And that she has never ceased to be. For thirty-seven years I awoke every morning to the smile that captivated me in Cambridge, when I handed her roses in the doorway of her walk-up. Betsey was the love of my life, and I have had no prouder yet more humbling sense of fulfillment than the knowledge that I was the love of hers.

With Betsey, my life was blessed.

Index

Page numbers in *italics* indicate illustrations

Index

About the Author

Eugene D. Genovese is the author of the groundbreaking classic *Roll, Jordan, Roll: The World the Slaves Made* as well as many other books. Several were coauthored with his late wife Elizabeth Fox-Genovese, including *The Mind of the Master Class: History and Faith in the Southern Slaveholders' Worldview* and *Slavery in White and Black: Class and Race in the Southern Slaveholders' New World Order.*